INCLUDES COMPLETE COVERAGE OF THE P-63 KINGCOBRA

63

P-39
Airacobra

A DETAIL & SCALE AVIATION PUBLICATION

in detail

Bert Kinzey

squadron/signal publications

COPYRIGHT © 1999 BY DETAIL & SCALE, INC.

This book is a product of Detail & Scale, Inc., which has sole responsibility for its content and layout, except that all contributors are responsible for the security clearance and copyright release of all materials submitted. Published by Squadron/Signal Publications, 1115 Crowley Drive, Carrollton, Texas 75011.

CONTRIBUTORS AND SOURCES:

Stan Piet
Frank Borman
Simon Brown
Holly Furster
Tony Corbo
Ron Blondell

Lloyd Jones
Bill Slatton
Jim Roeder
Jim Galloway
Stan Parker
Hans-Heiri Stapfer

Steve Benstead
Ricky Yokogawa
National Archives
Square One Aviation
Yanks Air Museum
United States Air Force Museum

Detail & Scale, Inc. and the author express a sincere word of thanks to Frank Borman for allowing detailed photographs of his beautifully restored P-63A Kingcobra to be taken specifically for this publication. Thanks are also extended to Simon Brown, Holly Furster, and Tony Corbo of Square One Aviation for making the aircraft available and open for photography.

Special thanks are also expressed to Ron Blondell of the Yanks Air Museum in Chino, California, for permitting detailed photography of the P-39N Airacobra being restored by the museum. Mr. Blondell also provided access to the museum's P-63C Kingcobra as well. The detailed coverage presented on the pages that follow would be far less extensive without the cooperation of Ron and his staff.

The United States Air Force Museum is also deserving of special thanks for granting the author permission and the opportunity to take detailed photographs of their P-39Q Airacobra. The Research Division at the museum also proved invaluable in providing information, photographs, and drawings of both the Airacobra and Kingcobra. Robert Spaulding and his volunteers were particularly helpful with the photography of the P-39Q, while David Menard provided considerable assistance during the original research for this publication.

Many photographs in this publication are credited to their contributors. Photographs with no credit indicated were taken by the author.

Above left, front cover photo: Colonel Edward S. Chickering flew this Airacobra named "SAGA BOY II" when he was the commanding officer of the 357th Fighter Group. It was the second P-39Q-1-BE to come off the production line. **(Piet collection)**

Above right, rear cover, top photo: Colors and details of the instrument panel in the Yanks Air Museum's P-39N are revealed in this large photograph. For additional color photos of this cockpit, see pages 38 and 39.

Right, rear cover, bottom photo: Square One Aviation did a flawless restoration of a P-63A for Frank Borman. They included a completely detailed nose compartment that matches exactly the factory specifications for Kingcobras as they left the assembly line. Additional photographs of the nose compartment in this aircraft can be found on page 45.

INTRODUCTION

The streamlined design and narrow cross section of the Airacobra's fuselage is emphasized in this front view of a P-39D-1-BE. This version of the Airacobra was fitted with the longer 20-mm cannon instead of the 37-mm weapon installed in most variants. Note also the alignment of the four wing guns. (National Archives)

Although it was one of the most brilliantly designed and engineered fighters of World War II, the P-39 Airacobra became one of the most controversial and disappointing American aircraft of that era. It was conceived as a fast interceptor designed around a hard hitting 37-mm cannon that fired explosive shells to insure the destruction of any enemy aircraft. But after promising flight tests by the XP-39, the U. S. Army Air Corps mandated that the turbo-supercharger be removed. This short sighted and ill advised decision, made by leaders schooled and experienced only in ground warfare, meant that the high altitude performance of the aircraft suffered considerably. But the aircraft's users, particularly the British, blamed Bell Aircraft for the substandard high altitude performance, and the Airacobra was not held in high favor by most of the pilots who flew it.

The cannon armament made it a most effective ground attack aircraft where high altitude performance was not a requirement. Using its cannon and machine guns, the Airacobra could destroy even armored targets, protected emplacements, and locomotives with relative ease. The Soviets used hundreds of P-39s against German ground forces with great effectiveness.

The supercharger was restored in a refined design named the P-63 Kingcobra, and high altitude performance increased significantly. Nevertheless, the Kingcobra was used almost exclusively in the ground attack role by the Russians and French. Kingcobras also served in the USAAF where they performed the unusual task of flying as manned targets for bomber crewmen who were learning the art of aerial gunnery. However, P-63s did not serve in combat with the USAAF.

Relatively little has been written about the Airacobra and Kingcobra, and what is available leaves out many interesting facts and details about these two aircraft. To provide the most detailed coverage possible, trips were made to photograph two P-39s and two P-63s. These include the P-39Q at the United States Air Force Museum at Dayton, Ohio, and the P-39N under restoration at the Yanks Air Museum in Chino, California. The P-39N was still under restoration when the photographs were taken, and many details were easily accessible including the cockpit, nose compartment, and engine bay.

The Yanks P-63C was also photographed in detail, as was the newly restored P-63A belonging to former astronaut Frank Borman. This Kingcobra was meticulously returned to original specifications by Square One Aviation at Chino, California, and the author was very fortunate to be able to take several dozen detailed photographs of this magnificent aircraft. Particularly noteworthy are the photos of the armament in the nose.

Lloyd Jones produced original 1/72nd scale drawings specifically for this publication, and they are the most accurate drawings of these two aircraft ever provided to the public. They show the correct depth of the fuselage and include details not found on other drawings.

For scale modelers, we have included our usual modeling summary on the last two pages of the book where information is provided about plastic model kits of the Airacobra and Kingcobra.

DEVELOPMENTAL HISTORY

In its original configuration, the XP-39 had a large intake for the supercharger on the left side of the fuselage. Also note the wide propeller blades and the higher canopy. *(National Archives)*

In 1935, Robert J. Woods, the chief design engineer for the newly formed Bell Aircraft Corporation, witnessed a firepower demonstration at the Army's Ordnance Proving Grounds at Aberdeen, Maryland. Of the weapons demonstrated, the most impressive was the American Armament Corporation's 37-mm cannon which was installed in Bell's first design, the FM-1 Airacuda. With aircraft becoming larger and sturdier in the 1930s, Woods also envisioned an interceptor that could carry this large weapon, because its explosive shell would insure destruction of the target. When the U. S. Army Air Corps issued specification X-609 for a new pursuit plane, Woods began work on his second design for Bell. He conceived a sleek single-engine interceptor designed around the powerful cannon. With a turbo-supercharged engine, he was also certain the aircraft would attain a top speed in excess of four-hundred miles per hour.

Woods believed the slow-firing weapon should be installed so that it fired through the propeller hub rather than being synchronized to fire through the arc of the propeller blades. The Germans were developing a similar concept using a 23-mm cannon in their Messerschmitt Bf 109, but they were placing the cannon in the V between the cylinders of the engine. There were no American engines that would permit this arrangement, so Woods decided to mount the engine aft of the cannon and machine gun armament and use a drive shaft to turn the propeller through a gear case just behind the hub.

In his original layout, Woods placed the cockpit behind the engine, and this design became known as Bell Model 3. A mockup in this configuration was displayed on May 24, 1937, but it became evident that the extreme aft location of the cockpit would result in very poor visibility for the pilot. Bell changed the design so that the engine was located behind the cockpit, but this meant using a much longer drive shaft that reached eight feet in length. Skeptics feared this arrangement would be more complex and therefore more prone to failure. In actual use, it proved to be very reliable. Pilots feared that the engine might tear lose of its mounts and slam forward into the cockpit in a crash, thus crushing the pilot to death. But again, operational use demonstrated

After wind tunnel tests at NACA's facility at Langley, Virginia, the aircraft was redesigned and redesignated the XP-39B. The USAAC also ordered that the supercharger be removed, thus severely reducing performance at high altitudes. The scoop for carburetion air was moved to a position behind the cockpit, and it would remain in this location on all production versions of the Airacobra that followed. *(National Archives)*

Thirteen YP-39 prototypes were produced and used for flight testing. They were almost identical to the redesigned XP-39B, and most had armament installed.

(USAFM)

that these fears were unfounded. The structural integrity of the airframe held the engine in place and the cockpit remained in tact.

On October 7, 1937, the USAAC ordered a single XP-39, serial number 38-326, and it was called Model 4 at Bell. With the cockpit located between the armament in the nose and the engine to the rear, the design offered excellent balance. The cross section of the fuselage was very narrow, because the widest part around the powerplant was at its center rather than in the nose. This streamlined design, along with the flush riveted skin, helped reduce drag and offer the promise of speeds in excess of the desired four hundred miles-per-hour.

The unusual layout also permitted the use of a tricycle landing gear with a wide tread that proved excellent for use on rough unprepared fields. When it was rolled out of Bell's factory, the Army was very impressed by the engineering of the XP-39. It was the smallest of all U. S. Army fighters used during World War II, and through the use of lightweight materials, gross weight was just over 6,000 pounds.

On April 6, 1938, Jimmy Taylor took the XP-39 up for its maiden flight from Wright Field, Ohio. With its turbo-supercharger, but without its armament and only partial fuel, the aircraft achieved a top speed of 390 mph at 20,000 feet. With some refinement of the design, it appeared that this could be easily increased to better than 400 miles-per-hour.

The aircraft underwent evaluation in the wind tunnels at the National Advisory Committee for Aeronautics' facilities at Langley, Virginia. The design was improved, and most noticeably, the canopy enclosure was lowered and streamlined. But in the interim, the Army had decided to delete the turbo-supercharger. Woods protested, stating that this would destroy the entire concept of the design and mean that the aircraft could not perform the interceptor role for which it was intended. The Army's leadership refused to listen. They believed that wars were fought on the ground and that aircraft were only to support and augment ground forces. Interceptors, which were intended to engage enemy bombers, were not a high priority, because America was protected by the vast oceans which surrounded it. These leaders were unable to see that interceptors would be needed to protect ground forces, installations, production facilities, and cities in any theater of operations. Further, the concept of air-to-air combat between fighters seemed unim-

portant and foreign to them. Instead, the decision makers in the Army wanted both bombers and fighters designed primarily to directly support their forces on the ground. Their decision to delete the turbo-supercharger from the XP-39 effectively changed the role of the aircraft from interceptor to ground support fighter.

With the design changes made and the turbo-supercharger removed, 38-326 was redesignated the XP-39B. Flight testing confirmed the expected loss of performance at altitudes above 15,000 feet. Beginning on October 12, 1940, thirteen YP-39 prototypes were delivered, and although it was planned that one of these be fitted with a turbo-supercharger and designated the YP-39A, these plans were canceled and all thirteen were completed without turbo-supercharging.

The first production version of the Airacobra was the P-39C. Eighty were in the initial order, but only twenty were completed as P-39Cs. These were used as service test aircraft with the 31st Pursuit Group at Selfridge Field, Michigan, and they differed from all other variants of the Airacobra in that they had two .30-caliber machine guns in the nose along with the two .50-caliber guns and the 37-mm cannon. The two nose-mounted .30-caliber machine guns would not be present on any subsequent versions.

Meanwhile, the French had ordered 200 Airacobras, but France fell to the Germans before these aircraft were delivered. The British took over the French order and placed their own order for an additional 475. They had originally intended to name them Caribous, but the RAF decided to use the American name instead. They opted for the faster firing Hispano 20-mm cannon with a higher muzzle velocity instead of the 37-mm cannon used in the American aircraft.

After taking delivery of their first few Airacobra Is, the RAF used them briefly in only one squadron before rejecting the remainder of the order. The British were very upset that the Airacobra did not live up to the performance promised by the turbo-supercharged XP-39. It seems inconceivable that they could have failed to understand that the USAAC's decision to remove the turbo-supercharger would result in a decrease in high altitude performance, yet they even accused Bell of operating in bad faith. But the problem clearly did not originate with Bell.

The first production version of the Airacobra was the P-39C, but only twenty were built. All armament was located in the nose, including the 37-mm cannon as well as two .50-caliber, and two .30-caliber machine guns.

(National Archives)

After the first twenty aircraft in the original order for eighty Airacobras were delivered as P-39Cs, the remaining sixty were completed as P-39Ds. This P-39D was assigned to the 31st Pursuit Group at Selfridge Field, Michigan. (USAFM)

The Soviet Union received 212 of the Airacobra Is that had been intended for the Royal Air Force, while the U. S. Army Air Forces retained 179. The USAAF designated the aircraft the P-400, and many were sent to the southwest Pacific where fighters of any kind were desperately needed.

By this time, the remaining sixty aircraft in the initial order for the U. S. Army had been delivered as P-39Ds. These were followed by P-39D-1-BEs and P-39D-2-BEs which were fitted with the 20-mm cannon like the Airacobra I and P-400. These P-39D-1-BEs and P-39D-2-BEs served in mixed squadrons with P-400s in the southwest Pacific during the early months of 1942.

The 8th Pursuit Group was the first unit to use the Airacobra in combat when it flew missions in March 1942. In May 1942, the "pursuit" name was replaced with "fighter," so "pursuit group" became "fighter group," and "pursuit squadron" became "fighter squadron." In July 1942, the 35th Fighter Group became the second unit to enter combat with Airacobras. They were soon followed by the 347th Fighter Group which operated Airacobra Is that were still painted in British camouflage and had RAF serial numbers on their aft fuselage sides. P-39D-1-BEs were also assigned to the 347th FG which began operations on Guadalcanal in August 1942. Their experience proved that the Airacobra was an excellent

dive bomber and ground attack aircraft, but it was not nearly the equal of the A6M Zero in aerial combat. The Airacobra's tricycle landing gear made it ideally suitable for operations on the rough strips on Guadalcanal and elsewhere in the Pacific.

The 54th Fighter Group, consisting of the 56th, 57th, and 42nd Fighter Squadrons, operated in Alaska until 1943. The 18th Fighter Squadron of the 343rd Fighter Group also participated in the fighting against the Japanese in the Aleutians.

On the other side of the world, Airacobras in the 33rd Fighter Squadron of the 342nd Composite Group were based in Iceland. The 31st, 81st, 332nd, 350th, and 354th Fighter Groups fought in Africa and Italy. Other groups which had Airacobras in their squadrons also served in the Canal Zone in Central America from 1941 through 1943. These included the 22nd and 23rd Fighter Squadrons of the 36th Fighter Group, the 52nd Fighter Squadron of the 32nd Fighter Group, and the 24th, 28th, 29th, 30th, 31st, 32nd, 43rd, and 51st Fighter Squadrons of the XXVI Fighter Command.

In addition to the squadrons and groups that served in combat, Airacobras were used in numerous training squadrons throughout the United States, and 4,746 were provided to the Soviet Union where they were used very successfully as ground attack aircraft. Australia and the Free French also flew Airacobras during the war, and some were even provided to Italian co-belligerent forces after the Italian Armistice in 1943. Eighteen USAAF P-39Ds from the 81st Fighter Group were interned by Portugal when operational problems forced them to land in the supposedly neutral country. These were subsequently operated by the Portugese Air Force.

Beginning with the Airacobra I/P-400 and the P-39D, the two .30-caliber machine guns in the nose were deleted, and four weapons of the same caliber were installed in the wings. This armament would remain the same on all subsequent Airacobra variants except the P-39Q. On this final version, the four .30-caliber machine guns were removed from the wings, and they were replaced by two gun pods under the wings, each of which contained a single .50-caliber machine gun.

Only minor changes differentiated the Airacobra versions between the P-39D and P-39Q. The primary change from one variant to the next was the version of

The P-39N was the last of four "mid-series" versions of the Airacobra which also included the P-39K, P-39L, and P-39M. Originally ordered as P-39Gs, these aircraft were divided among these four variants as production continued. "ILL WINDS" was a P-39N-1-BE photographed at Gray Field, Washington. (National Archives)

The final and definitive version of the Airacobra was the P-39Q. It was also built in the greatest numbers of any variant, with a total of 4,905 being delivered. The .30-caliber wing guns were replaced with a gun pod containing a single .50-caliber machine gun under each wing. (National Archives)

the Allison V-1710 engine that was installed, and on some variants, the internal fuel capacity was decreased. Other changes were minor, and these are addressed in more detail on the pages that follow.

Early experience with the Airacobra clearly illustrated the error of the Army's decision to remove the turbo-supercharger. In February 1941, an improved design was proposed, and work began on what would become the P-63 Kingcobra. Much of the information used in its development came from the testing of three XP-39Es. A single XP-63 was ordered on June 27, 1941, but a second one was added later. Both were converted from XP-39Es, while an XP-63A was built from the ground up. The first XP-63 made its maiden flight on December 7, 1942, with Bell chief test pilot Robert M. Stanley at the controls. In making this flight, the Kingcobra became the only U. S. fighter to make its first flight after America entered the war and then be produced in large numbers while the war continued.

The P-63 not only had a hydraulic turbocharger, but laminar flow wings were also a new feature. The tail was redesigned, and all were fitted with a four-blade propeller. Ailerons and elevators were covered with a metal skin, but the rudder remained fabric covered. The Kingcobra was also larger than the Airacobra, and access panels were redesigned to ease maintenance and loading of the weapons.

There were two major production versions of the Kingcobra, and the first of these was the P-63A of which 1,725 were built. The XP-63B was canceled, and 1,227 P-63Cs followed. These could be differentiated from the earlier P-63As by the long fin faired into the lower aft fuselage to increase longitudinal stability. Both versions were capable of a maximum speed in excess of four-hundred miles per hour, placing the Kingcobra in the same speed class as other front line fighters of the day. Coverage of the individual variants of the Kingcobra begins on page 56.

In the United States, many Kingcobras were used in the highly unusual role of manned targets. With a thicker skin, special armor, and a redundant pitot system, these aircraft were flown against bombers in mock attacks. Gunners in the bombers fired frangible bullets at the target aircraft, and these bullets simply disintegrated harmlessly into dust when they hit the Kingcobra target aircraft. Lights would flash on the skin of the target to let the gunners know when they scored hits. This feature lead to the target aircraft being called "Pinballs." While it might have been a rather disconcerting mission for a pilot to fly, evidence indicates that flying these aircraft as targets was no more dangerous than any other training sortie. In addition to being manned targets, these aircraft were also used to tow targets that were fired on with real bullets.

No P-63s ever saw combat with USAAF squadrons, but 2,421 of the 3,303 built were delivered to the Soviet Union under the Lend-Lease Act. The Soviets used them very effectively as ground attack and close support aircraft as they advanced on Germany from the east. Another three hundred were provided to the French, and some of these Kingcobras were still around to see action in Indochina during 1948.

Neither the Airacobra nor the Kingcobra gained the fame or glory bestowed on many other U. S. fighters used during World War II. Much criticism was leveled against the Airacobra in particular, but it was not the fault of the Bell designers or the aircraft itself. When the leadership of the U. S. Army decided to remove the turbo-supercharger from the XP-39, they also removed any possibility that the aircraft could serve in the interceptor role for which it was designed and for which it held so much promise. After being resigned to low altitude operations, the P-39 became one of the very best ground attack aircraft of the war. Once supercharging was restored in the redesigned and improved P-63 Kingcobra, the aircraft had significantly enhanced high altitude performance, but it remained a primary ground attack aircraft in the Soviet Air Force. It could be said that the Airacobras and Kingcobras were the A-10 Warthogs of World War II. They may not have received the glory, but they did an important and thankless job that had to be done.

No P-63s saw combat with the USAAF, but specially modified and armored Kingcobras provided realistic training as target aircraft for gunners in bombers. By using frangible bullets, which harmlessly disintegrated when they hit the target aircraft, the gunners were able to improve their accuracy before having to fire shots in combat. **(USAFM)**

Of the 3,303 Kingcobras built, 2,421 were delivered to the Soviet Union. The Russians used both Airacobras and Kingcobras extensively as ground attack aircraft in combat against the Germans. They were painted in the standard USAAF Olive Drab over Neutral Gray camouflage scheme. The French also received 300 Kingcobras. **(Roeder collection)**

XFL-1 AIRABONITA

The XFL-1 Airabonita shared many common features with the Airacobra, but it was not simply another version of the P-39. It was marginally smaller and lighter, and it had a conventional landing gear arrangement. Because of the conventional gear, the air scoops for the oil coolers had to be moved from the leading edge of the wing roots to a position under the wings as seen in this view.

(Jones collection)

In an effort to produce a carrier-based fighter for the U. S. Navy, the Bell Aircraft Company created the XFL-1 based on the Airacobra's design. A single experimental aircraft was ordered by the Navy on November 8, 1938, and it was assigned the Bureau Number 1588. Named the Airabonita, the XFL-1 became the first aircraft in the U. S. Navy to have a liquid-cooled inline engine since 1928. Brian Sparks took the aircraft up for its first flight on May 13, 1940.

Although there were several obvious design similarities between the XFL-1 and the XP-39B, there were even more differences. The Airabonita's wingspan was wider and its chord was greater. The fuselage was shorter, and the canopy was higher to provide better visibility for carrier landings. But the most noticeable difference was the conventional landing gear arrangement necessitated for carrier operations of that day. This change also required several other modifications to the design. The conventional gear arrangement meant that the center of balance had to be shifted aft, and this was accomplished by moving the main gear struts forward. But in doing so, the wheel wells had to be located where the ducts for the inlets were in the wing roots. These ducts, which supplied air to the oil coolers and the radiator for the engine coolant, had to be deleted, and they were replaced with scoops under the fuselage.

The Allison XV-1710-6 powerplant was chosen for the XFL-1, but no supercharging was included. Armament was initially to include a 23-mm Madsen cannon and two .30-caliber machine guns, but this was later changed to one .50-caliber gun in the propeller hub and two .30-caliber guns firing through the arc of the propeller. In any event, no armament was ever installed.

The XFL-1 Airabonita was a relatively small lightweight fighter, and its planned armament was considered inadequate. The success of the heavier and far more powerful Chance Vought XF4U Corsair, which became the first fighter to exceed 400 miles-per-hour in level flight, made the choice easy for the Navy, and the Airabonita program was terminated.

The success of the heavier and more powerful Chance Vought F4U Corsair resulted in the cancellation of the XFL-1 project. It became the last aircraft delivered to the U. S. Navy with vertical red, white, and blue stripes on the rudder. *(Jones collection)*

DATA

Version	XFL-1
Number Built	1
Armament (Not Installed)	1 x .50 caliber MG, 2 x .30 caliber MG
Powerplant	Allison V-1710-6
Horsepower	1,150
Maximum Speed	338 mph at 11,000 feet
Rate of Climb	3.8 minutes to 10,000 feet
Ceiling	30,900 feet
Maximum Range	1,072 miles
Combat Range	965 miles
Wingspan	35 feet
Length	29 feet, 9 inches
Height	12 feet, 9.5 inches
Empty Weight	5,161 pounds
Gross Weight	6,651 pounds
Maximum Take-off Weight	7,212 pounds

P-39 AIRACOBRA VARIANTS
XP-39

In its original configuration, the XP-39 had a much higher framed cockpit enclosure than it did after it was redesigned following wind tunnel tests at NACA's facility at Langley, Virginia. (USAFM)

Once it was decided to place the engine behind the cockpit, the lone XP-39, 38-326, was built in Bell's plant in Buffalo, New York. After completion, it was shipped to Wright Field, Ohio, where its first flight was made on April 6, 1938. Powered by a turbo-supercharged Allison V-1710-17 engine which produced 1,150 horsepower, it attained a top speed of 390 miles-per-hour at 20,000 feet. This was very promising, although it was accomplished with no armament installed, and the fuel tanks were only partially filled.

As originally designed and flown, the XP-39 had a high canopy with thin frames that looked much like a greenhouse. Scoops for the turbo-supercharger, the oil coolers, and the radiator for the engine coolant were located on the sides of the fuselage. The fuselage itself was built in two major sections, with the forward part including the nose, cockpit, and engine bay containing the structural mounts for the powerplant. The aft section was simply covered stringers leading back to the tail. Radio gear was installed inside the aft fuselage.

The early flights indicated that the performance of the aircraft was promising, and it was believed that it could be improved by redesigning the airframe. As a result, the XP-39 was moved from Wright Field to the full scale wind tunnels at the National Advisory Committee on Aeronautics' facility at Langley, Virginia. Testing in these huge wind tunnels led to a major redesign of the airframe that resulted in the XP-39B.

The large scoop for the supercharger and the smaller vertical tail are visible in this left rear view. (USAFM)

DATA

Version	XP-39
Bell Model Number	11
Number Built	1
Armament	None
Powerplant	Allison V-1710-17
Horsepower	1,150
Maximum Speed	390 mph at 20,000 feet
Rate of Climb	5 minutes to 20,000 feet
Ceiling	32,000 feet
Maximum Range	1,400 miles
Combat Range	390 miles
Wingspan	35 feet, 10 inches
Length	28 feet, 8 inches
Height	11 feet
Empty Weight	3,995 pounds
Gross Weight	5,550 pounds
Maximum Take-off Weight	6,204 pounds
Maximum Internal Fuel	200 gallons
Maximum External Fuel	None

XP-39B

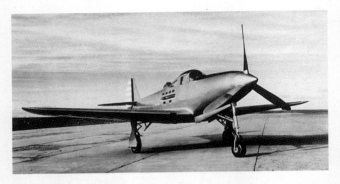

After wind tunnel tests, the XP-39 was redesigned, and the result was the sleek streamlined appearance that was carried forward on all subsequent production Airacobras. The wingspan was decreased and the fuselage was lengthened. The designation of the aircraft was changed to XP-39B after it was redesigned. (USAFM)

The scoops for the oil coolers were moved from the right side of the fuselage to the wing roots. Also note the large door on the front of the nose landing gear strut. This original design was later replaced with a small door at the top of the strut and two longer doors on each side of the gear well. (USAFM)

The wind tunnel tests on the XP-39 at Langley, Virginia, indicated that a number of changes to the aircraft's airframe would be beneficial and improve performance. As a result, the wingspan was reduced from 35' 10" to 34' 0", and the length of the fuselage was increased from 28' 8" to 29' 9". The canopy was lowered, to reduce drag, and its framework was strengthened. The scoops for the oil coolers and engine coolant radiator were removed from the fuselage sides and replaced with inlets that were buried in the wing roots. Two different arrangements for the nose gear doors were tried, with the first being a long door attached to the front of the strut. This was later replaced with a small door on the strut and two longer doors on the sides of the well. Inner doors were also added to the main gear wells to completely enclose the gear when it was retracted.

The greatest effect on the aircraft's performance was caused not by changes made as a result of the wind tunnel testing, but by a decision by the Army to delete the B-5 turbo-supercharger. Believing that the primary purpose of both bombers and fighters was to support troops on the ground, Army leaders placed little emphasis on high altitude performance. They wanted the new aircraft to use its cannon and machine guns against ground targets rather than enemy aircraft. By deleting the supercharger, they eliminated any chance that the Airacobra would be the effective interceptor it was designed to be. The engine was changed from the V-1710-17 to the V-1710-37 which produced 1,090 horsepower at 13,300 feet.

The first flight of the redesigned aircraft, now designated the XP-39B, was made on November 25, 1939. In spite of the streamlined design, top speed dropped to only 375 miles-per-hour, and this was at 15,000 feet instead of 20,000 feet where the original XP-39 had reached 390 miles-per-hour. But the die had been cast, and the thirteen YP-39 prototypes and all production versions of the Airacobra were to fly without the benefit of a supercharged powerplant.

On the XP-39B, there were no scoops on the sides of the fuselage, but there were a series of cooling louvers around the exhaust ports on the right side. The scoop for carburetion air was moved to its permanent location on the spine just aft of the cockpit. It is smaller than the one that would appear later on production aircraft. (USAFM)

DATA

Version	XP-39B
Bell Model Number	11
Number Built	1*
Armament	None
Powerplant	Allison V-1710-37
Horsepower	1,090
Maximum Speed	375 mph at 15,000 feet
Rate of Climb	7.5 minutes to 20,000 feet
Ceiling	36,000 feet
Maximum Range	1,400 miles
Combat Range	600 miles
Wingspan	34 feet
Length	29 feet, 9 inches
Height	9 feet, 3 inches
Empty Weight	4,955 pounds
Gross Weight	5,834 pounds
Maximum Take-off Weight	6,450 pounds
Maximum Internal Fuel	200 gallons
Maximum External Fuel	None

* This was the XP-39 airframe that was redesigned after wind tunnel tests at the NACA facility in Langley, Virginia.

YP-39

Thirteen YP-39 prototypes were built for flight tests and other evaluation. They were delivered in a natural metal finish with the national insignia in all four wing positions and red, white, and blue stripes on the tail. **(USAFM)**

On April 27, 1939, the USAAC ordered thirteen YP-39 prototypes. Originally, one of these was to be fitted with a supercharger and designated the YP-39A, but this plan was canceled, and all thirteen were delivered without superchargers. Army serial numbers 40-27 through 40-39 were assigned. Like the XP-39B, they had the V-1710-37 engine which produced 1,090 horsepower. The first YP-39 had no armament installed, but most of the remaining twelve had armament including the 37-mm cannon, two .50-caliber machine guns, and two .30-caliber guns, all of which were located in the nose.

The first YP-39 made its initial flight on September 13, 1940, and it was turned over to the USAAC on October 12. With the additional weight of the armament, top speed decreased further to only 368 miles-per-hour at 15,000 feet.

The YP-39s were delivered in a natural metal finish with national insignias in all four wing positions. There were no national insignias on the fuselage sides. Red, white, and blue stripes were painted on the vertical tail and rudder, as was standard for U. S. military aircraft in the late 1930s and into 1940 and 1941. **U. S. ARMY** was stenciled in large flat black letters under the wings.

Like the XP-39B, the YP-39s had a single air scoop in the leading edge of each wing for the oil coolers and engine coolant radiator. **(USAFM)**

DATA

Version	YP-39
Bell Model Number	12
Number Built	13
Armament	1 X 37-mm cannon, 2 x .50 caliber MG, 2 x .30 caliber MG
Powerplant	Allison V-1710-37
Horsepower	1,090
Maximum Speed	368 mph at 13,600 feet
Rate of Climb	7.3 minutes to 20,000 feet
Ceiling	33,300 feet
Maximum Range	1,000 miles
Combat Range	600 miles
Wingspan	34 feet
Length	30 feet, 2 inches
Height	11 feet, 10 inches
Empty Weight	5,042 pounds
Gross Weight	7,180 pounds
Maximum Take-off Weight	7,235 pounds
Maximum Internal Fuel	170 gallons
Maximum External Fuel	None

P-39C

Many details of the P-39C are revealed in this excellent view. The landing gear struts are a steel color rather than the Bell green color used on later aircraft. The front of each propeller blade is also an unpainted steel color. The original nose gear wheel had a small diameter with a larger tire than late production versions of the Airacobra. There were no machine guns in the wings of the P-39C.
(Jones collection)

Armorers load the two .50-caliber and two .30-caliber machine guns in the nose of a P-39C. The ammunition box for the right .30-caliber gun can be seen inside the bay. It was mounted forward of the box for the right .50-caliber machine gun. The P-39C was the only variant of the Airacobra to have the .30-caliber machine guns in the nose.
(USAFM)

The initial production order by the USAAC for Airacobras included eighty aircraft. Originally called P-45s, the designation was changed to P-39C for political reasons. Production began in 1940, but only twenty of the eighty aircraft had been delivered when the improved P-39D replaced the P-39C on the assembly line.

The first flight by a P-39C was made in January 1941, and most of the twenty P-39Cs were assigned to the 40th Pursuit Squadron of the 31st Pursuit Group at Selfridge Field, Michigan, where they were used as service test aircraft. They were very similar to the YP-39s, but they were powered by the V-1710-35 engine with six exhaust stubs on each side. They also had armored glass behind the windshield. Like the prototypes, they had the 37-mm cannon, two .50-caliber and two .30-caliber machine guns in the nose compartment.

The P-39Cs were the first Airacobras delivered in the standard Olive Drab over Neutral Gray paint scheme, and they had national insignias on both fuselage sides and the upper left and lower right wing positions. **U. S. ARMY** was stenciled in large black letters under the wings, however, they did not have the red, white, and blue stripes on the vertical tail and rudder that had been applied to the natural metal YP-39s and which remained on many operational U. S. military aircraft in early 1941. Initially, aircraft numbers on the nose and tail, as well as the **31P** indicating the pursuit group to which they were assigned, were lettered with yellow paint, but this was later changed to flat black before the end of 1941.

No P-39Cs were used in combat, and they were subsequently redesignated RP-39Cs to denote a restricted non-combat status.

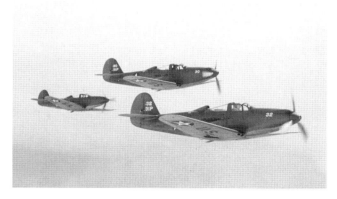

Beginning with the P-39C, there were two smaller inlets in each wing root rather than the larger single inlet as found on the YP-39. Also note the fully enclosed retracted landing gear, the navigation lights on the wing tips, and the retractable landing light under the left wing. P-39Cs were the first Airacobras delivered in the standard USAAF camouflage of Olive Drab over Neutral Gray. They had national insignias on the top left and bottom right wing positions, as well as on both sides of the aft fuselage. U. S. ARMY was painted under the wings.

(National Archives)

Most of the twenty P-39Cs were assigned to the 40th Pursuit Squadron of the 31st Pursuit Group based at Selfridge Field, Michigan. They were used as service test and evaluation aircraft, and they often flew with their armament removed.

(USAFM)

DATA

Version	P-39C
Bell Model Number	13
Number Built	20
Armament	1 X 37-mm cannon, 2 x .50 caliber MG, 2 x .30 caliber MG
Powerplant	Allison V-1710-35
Horsepower	1,150
Maximum Speed	379 mph at 13,000 feet
Rate of Climb	3.9 minutes to 12,000 feet
Ceiling	33,200 feet
Maximum Range	730 miles
Combat Range	450 miles
Wingspan	34 feet
Length	30 feet, 2 inches
Height	11 feet, 10 inches
Empty Weight	5,070 pounds
Gross Weight	7,180 pounds
Maximum Take-off Weight	7,300 pounds
Maximum Internal Fuel	170 gallons
Maximum External Fuel	None

Ground crew personnel maneuver a P-39C into its parking spot on Selfridge Field. Unit markings consisted only of a yellow aircraft number on the nose and tail and a yellow 31P on the vertical tail indicating the 31st Pursuit Group.

(National Archives)

P-39C 1/72nd SCALE DRAWING

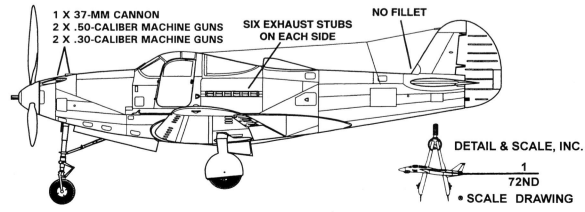

1 X 37-MM CANNON
2 X .50-CALIBER MACHINE GUNS
2 X .30-CALIBER MACHINE GUNS

SIX EXHAUST STUBS ON EACH SIDE

NO FILLET

DETAIL & SCALE, INC.

1
72ND
SCALE DRAWING

DETAIL & SCALE, 1/72nd SCALE, COPYRIGHT © DRAWING BY LLOYD S. JONES

AIRACOBRA I & P-400

The first Airacobra I is ready for delivery to the Royal Air Force. After the British canceled most of their order, many Airacobra Is were delivered to the USAAF where they were given the P-400 designation. (Piet collection)

On April 30, 1940, the French placed an order for 200 Airacobras, but Germany defeated France before any of these aircraft could be delivered. The RAF took over the French order and added it to their own orders for 475

Still painted in its British camouflage colors, a P-400 from the 67th Fighter Squadron of the 347th Fighter Group is readied for a flight on Guadalcanal. (USAFM)

Bell Model 12s. But the British specified that the 37-mm cannon be replaced with a Hispano 20-mm cannon, trading the larger and heavier shell for a higher muzzle velocity and faster rate of fire. Sixty rounds of ammunition were carried for the weapon. Additionally, the RAF stipulated that there would only be two .303-caliber machine guns in the nose, but an additional four guns of the same caliber would be added in the wings. Originally, the British intended to name the aircraft the Caribou, but they ultimately decided to used the American name, Airacobra. The RAF assigned serials AH728 through AH738, AP266 through AP283, BW100 through BW183, and BX135 through BX174.

The British claimed to have based their order on the interceptor specifications including a top speed of 400 miles-per-hour and a ceiling of 36,000 feet. But the Airacobra Is had the V-1710-35 powerplant without supercharging. It produced only 1,150 horsepower and delivered a top speed of 367 miles-per-hour. Unlike the V-1710-35s used in the P-39C, these engines had twelve exhaust stubs on each side.

After receiving a few Airacobra Is and assigning them to No. 601 Squadron, the British canceled their order for all remaining Airacobra Is, blaming Bell for deceiving them and operating in bad faith concerning the aircraft's performance. But it was the U. S. Army's decision to delete the supercharger from the Airacobra that had caused the drop in performance rather than anything Bell had done. In fact, Bell had adamantly protested the deletion of the supercharger. Clearly, the British were

World War II.

By the time America entered the war, the USAAF was desperate for combat aircraft of all types. They took delivery of 179 of the Airacobra Is originally destined for the RAF and gave them the P-400 designation. Over 100 of these were rushed to Australia where they were mixed with P-39D-1-BE and P-39D-2-BEs in some of the first American fighter groups to see action against the Japanese. The need for the P-400s was so immediate that they were operated in USAAF squadrons still painted in their British camouflage schemes and carrying RAF serial numbers. Among the groups to utilize the P-400s in combat were the 8th Fighter Group in Australia and New Guinea, the 35th Fighter Group in New Guinea, and the 347th Fighter Group on Guadalcanal.

Ground crew personnel work on a P-400 under a net in the austere conditions of Guadalcanal early in the war. With the Japanese still on the island, it was not uncommon to find these mechanics working with a sidearm strapped on their hip. **(USAFM)**

DATA

Version	Airacobra I/P-400
Bell Model Number	14
Number Built	675
Armament	1 X 20-mm cannon, 2 x .50 caliber MG, 4 x .30 caliber MG
Powerplant	Allison V-1710-35
Horsepower	1,150
Maximum Speed	358 mph at 15,000 feet
Rate of Climb	5.1 minutes to 10,000 feet
Ceiling	29,000 feet
Maximum Range	1,098 miles
Combat Range	600 miles
Wingspan	34 feet
Length	30 feet, 2 inches
Height	9 feet, 3.25 inches
Empty Weight	5,360 pounds
Gross Weight	7,380 pounds
Maximum Take-off Weight	8,200 pounds
Maximum Internal Fuel	120 gallons
Maximum External Fuel	95 gallons

aware that the supercharger had been deleted by direction of the U. S. Army, and therefore performance would be reduced accordingly. It is apparent that their displayed surprise and disgust with the Airacobra I was more of an excuse to cancel the order than a legitimate reason to do so.

If the British didn't want the Airacobra Is they had ordered, the Soviet Union welcomed them enthusiastically. Fighting the Germans in intense battles on a wide front and around some of their major cities, the Russians made good use of the ground attack capabilities of the 212 Airacobra Is that were supplied to them from the British order. These became the first Airacobras used by the Soviets, and this led to their requests for many more P-39s and P-63 Kingcobras throughout the remainder of

AIRACOBRA I & P-400 1/72nd SCALE DRAWING

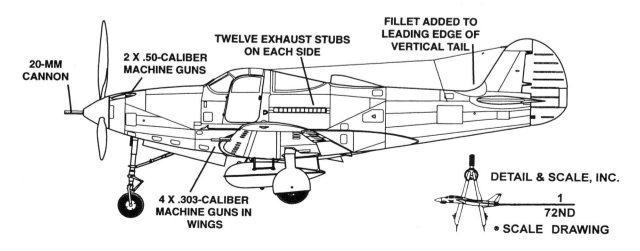

20-MM CANNON

2 X .50-CALIBER MACHINE GUNS

TWELVE EXHAUST STUBS ON EACH SIDE

FILLET ADDED TO LEADING EDGE OF VERTICAL TAIL

4 X .303-CALIBER MACHINE GUNS IN WINGS

DETAIL & SCALE, INC.

1
72ND
● SCALE DRAWING

DETAIL & SCALE, 1/72nd SCALE, COPYRIGHT © DRAWING BY LLOYD S. JONES

P-39D

Lt. John C. Robertson waves from the cockpit to signal that he is ready to taxi to the runway at Nachitoches Airport, Louisiana. The P-39D is assigned to the 39th Pursuit Squadron of the 31st Pursuit Group which participated in war games in Louisiana during late 1941.
(National Archives)

The final sixty aircraft in the original order for eighty Airacobras were completed as P-39D-BEs. These differed from the twenty P-39Cs in that they deleted the two .30-caliber machine guns from the nose, but four .30-caliber machine guns were added in the wings in the same arrangement as the .303-caliber guns in the Airacobra I. This required a strengthening of the wing structure to accommodate the weight of the guns and their ammunition. The added weight was substantial, because 1,000 rounds were provided for each gun, therefore a total of 2,000 rounds were carried in each wing in addition to the weight of the guns and their mounts. The P-39D-BEs were also fitted with self-sealing fuel tanks and additional armor plate to make them more combat worthy. A centerline bomb rack was added under the fuselage to carry an external fuel tank or a 250 or 500-pound bomb. Like the earlier P-39Cs, the P-39D-BEs were powered by the V-1710-35 engine which usually had six exhaust stubs on each side. However, photographic evidence proves that some had twelve stubs on each side.

Following the sixty P-39D-BEs, 705 P-39D-1-BEs were produced. These were identical to the P-39Ds except that the 37-mm cannon was replaced with a 20-mm cannon as installed on the Airacobra I/P-400. The P-39D-1-BE was also the first version of the Airacobra to have a fillet added at the base of the vertical tail as a production feature. This remained standard on all subsequent Airacobra variants, and some earlier aircraft had the fillet retrofitted. An additional 158 P-39D-2-BEs followed, and these differed from the P-39D-1-BEs only in that they were powered by a V-1710-63 engine that produced 1,325 horsepower. P-39D-1-BEs and P-39D-2-BEs served in mixed squadrons with the similar P-400s in the Pacific, and along with the P-400s, they were the first American Airacobras to see combat. Others were provided to the Soviet Union under the Lend-Lease Act.

Some earlier production D-models were modified for the photographic reconnaissance role with the addition or a K-24 and a K-25 camera mounted inside the aft fuselage. Armor was added around the oil coolers and the radiator for the engine coolant. Twenty-six of these were redesignated P-39D-3-BEs, and an additional eleven were called P-39D-4-BEs. All thirty-seven retained the original V-1710-35 engine.

Another of the 31st Pursuit Group's P-39Ds is shown at its home base of Selfridge Field, Michigan. Markings were the same as for the unit's early P-39Cs, except that the aircraft numbers and the 31P were painted in flat black instead of yellow. The unit's badge has been added to the door on each side. *(USAFM)*

P-39D-1-BEs were essentially the same as the P-39D, except that they were fitted with a 20-mm cannon instead of the 37-mm gun. P-39D-1-BEs often operated in mixed squadrons with P-400s, which also used the 20-mm cannon. (National Archives)

DATA

Version P-39D
Bell Model Number (P-39D-BE) 15
Bell Model Number (P-39D-1-BE & P-39-2-BE) . . . 14A

P-39D-1-BEs from the 362nd Fighter Squadron of the 357th Fighter Group participated in training exercises at Tonapah, Nevada, during the Spring of 1943. (Olmestead, via Roeder)

Number Built (P-39D) 60
Number Built (P-39D-1-BE) 705
Number Built (P-39D-2-BE) 158
Armament . . . . . 1 X 37-mm cannon*, 2 x .50 caliber
MG, 4 x .30 caliber MG
Powerplant:
    P-39D & P-39D-1-BE . . . . Allison V-1710-35
    P-39B-2-BE . . . . Allison V-1710-63
Horsepower:
    Allison V-1710-35 1,150
    Allison V-1710-63 1,325
Maximum Speed . . . . 368 mph at 12,000 feet**
Rate of Climb . . . . 5.7 minutes to 15,000 feet**
Ceiling . . . . 32,100 feet**
Maximum Range . . . . 1,545 miles**
Combat Range . . . . 800 miles**
Wingspan . . . . 34 feet
Length . . . . 30 feet, 2 inches
Height . . . . 11 feet, 10 inches
Empty Weight . . . . 6,300 pounds
Gross Weight . . . . 7,830 pounds
Maximum Take-off Weight . . . . 8,200 pounds
Maximum Internal Fuel . . . . 120 gallons
Maximum External Fuel . . . . 95 gallons***

* The P-39D-1-BE and P-39D-2-BE had a 20-mm cannon in place of the 37-mm cannon.

** Performance figures are for the P-39D.

*** The P-39D-2-BE could carry 175 gallons of external fuel.

1. Altimeter
2. Turn Indicator
3. Airspeed Indicator
4. Manifold Pressure
5. Clock
6. Ammeter
7. Liquidometer
8. Ignition Switch
9. Pressure Gage Gear Box
10. Air Temperature
11. Compass
12. Flight Indicator
13. Rate of Climb Indicator
14. Turn and Bank Indicator
15. Tachometer
16. Engine Gage Unit
17. Carburetor Air Temperature
18. Oxygen Regulator
19. Fuel Pressure Gage
20. Prestone Temperature
21. Suction Gage

Features of the instrument panel in a P-39D are indicated on this photograph. Keys are provided to the right of the photo. (USAFM)

Below: Details of the seat are shown in this drawing from the technical manual for the Airacobra. This seat was used in all versions of the P-39.

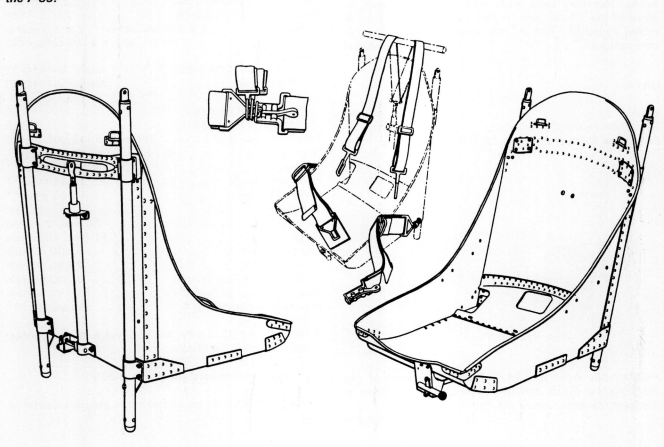

ARMAMENT DETAILS

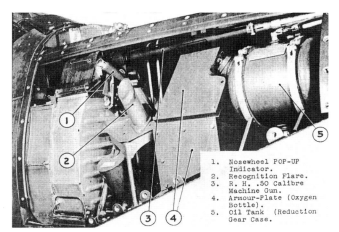

1. Nosewheel POP-UP Indicator.
2. Recognition Flare.
3. R. H. .50 Calibre Machine Gun.
4. Armour-Plate (Oxygen Bottle).
5. Oil Tank (Reduction Gear Case.

With the .30-caliber machine guns deleted from the nose, the gun bay in the P-39D was different from that in the P-39C. Armor plate for the oxygen bottle is where the ammunition box for the right .30-caliber machine gun had been in the P-39C. *(USAFM)*

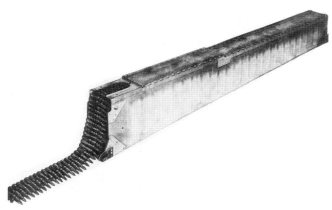

Two .30-caliber machine guns were added in each wing beginning with the P-39D. The outer gun was staggered further aft and slightly lower than the inboard gun. This is a front view of the guns in the left wing. *(USAFM)*

Two long boxes in each outer wing panel held the ammunition for the four .30-caliber machine guns, and 1,000 rounds could be carried for each gun. This permitted a very long firing time for these weapons. *(USAFM)*

P-39D-1-BE 1/72nd SCALE DRAWING

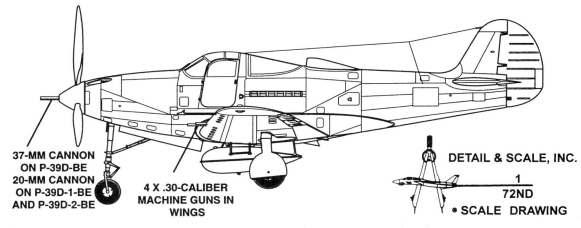

37-MM CANNON ON P-39D-BE 20-MM CANNON ON P-39D-1-BE AND P-39D-2-BE

4 X .30-CALIBER MACHINE GUNS IN WINGS

DETAIL & SCALE, INC.

$\frac{1}{72ND}$ SCALE DRAWING

DETAIL & SCALE, 1/72nd SCALE, COPYRIGHT © DRAWING BY LLOYD S. JONES

P-39F & P-39J

The P-39F was essentially the same as the previous P-39D, but it was fitted with an Aeroproducts propeller that was 10' 4" in diameter. By the time the P-39Fs were rolling off the production lines, the landing gear struts were painted the Bell green color. Note the unpainted, stainless steel, blast tubes on the .30-caliber wing guns. **(USAFM)**

The P-39F was very similar to the previous P-39D, and it also had the V-1710-35 powerplant that was used in most D-models. However, the engines used in the P-39F had twelve exhaust stubs on each side like those in the Airacobra I/P-400. The P-39F also marked a return to the 37-mm cannon after the 20-mm cannon had been installed in the Airacobra Is/P-400s, P-39D-1-BEs, and P-39D-2-BEs. The 37-mm cannon would be installed in all subsequent Airacobra variants. The Curtiss Electric propeller, used on early production Airacobras, was replaced by an Aeroproducts propeller with a diameter of 10' 4".

Twenty-seven P-39Fs were modified to carry two cameras in the aft fuselage in the same configuration used earlier on the P-39D-3-BEs and P-39D-4-BEs. The P-39Fs converted for the photographic reconnaissance role were redesignated P-39F-2-BEs.

Production of P-39Fs totaled 229 aircraft in an order of 244. The final twenty-five were completed with the V-1710-59 engine which had automatic boost control, and they were given the P-39J designation to distinguish them from the P-39Fs. Many P-39Fs and P-39Js were sent to Africa, while others replaced older versions of the Airacobra in the Aleutians and southwest Pacific.

Some references state that the P-39F had twelve exhaust stubs on each side, and while this was generally true, some had the arrangement with only six stubs as seen here on 41-7246. This aircraft also has a stub mast on the spine just aft of the scoop. **(USAFM)**

P-39F, 41-7224, has the twelve exhaust stubs on each side, and this was the more common arrangement found on P-39Fs. Interestingly, this Airacobra has its tail number repeated on its nose. This flying shot clearly shows the depth of the fuselage at its center. **(USAFM)**

Above: The last twenty-five aircraft in the P-39F order were completed with the V-1710-59 engine, and they were designated P-39Js. Externally, they were the same as the P-39Fs, and they had twelve exhaust stubs on each side. **(USAFM)**

Right: Lt. Leslie Spoonts flew this P-39J while he was assigned to the 57th Fighter Squadron of the 54th Fighter Group in Alaska. Three kill markings were painted on the left side just forward of the door. A color profile of this aircraft appears on page 33. **(USAFM)**

P-39F 1/72nd SCALE DRAWING

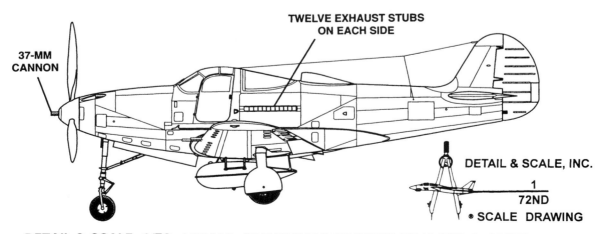

37-MM CANNON

TWELVE EXHAUST STUBS ON EACH SIDE

DETAIL & SCALE, INC.

$$\frac{1}{72ND}$$

SCALE DRAWING

DETAIL & SCALE, 1/72nd SCALE, COPYRIGHT © DRAWING BY LLOYD S. JONES

P-39K, P-39L, P-39M, & P-39N

The P-39K was the first of four "mid-series" variants of the Airacobra. These were originally ordered as P-39Gs, but they were divided into the four different versions when relatively minor changes were made as production continued. **(National Archives)**

Originally, 1,800 P-39Gs were ordered, but this designation was dropped, and the aircraft were delivered as P-39Ks, P-39Ls, P-39Ms, and P-39Ns. These four variants were commonly known as "mid-series" Airacobras.

The P-39K, of which 210 were built, had a V-1710-63 engine optimized for low altitude operations, and the Aeroproducts propeller continued to be used. This powerplant produced 1,325 horsepower and had six exhaust ports on each side. The ammunition for the .50-caliber machine guns in the nose was increased by fifteen rounds per gun. Six of the P-39Ks had two cameras added in the aft fuselage for the photo reconnaissance mission, and these were redesignated P-39K-1-BEs.

A total of 250 P-39Ls were produced under the same contract as the P-39K. This version returned to the Curtiss Electric propeller, and triangular shaped vents were added on each side of the nose to help discharge gun gasses before they could leak into the cockpit. The redesigned nose wheel also first appeared on the P-39L. The wheel was larger in diameter than the one used on earlier Airacobras, and the tire had lower walls so that the overall diameter remained the same. This wheel and tire arrangement was more aerodynamic so it offered less drag. The vents and the redesigned nose wheel remained standard on the subsequent variants of the Airacobra.

A top view of the same P-39K shown above provides a good look at the planform of the Airacobra's wings and horizontal tail surfaces. **(National Archives)**

Eleven of the 250 P-39Ls were converted to carry two cameras in the same way earlier versions had been, and these were redesignated P-39L-2-BEs.

The P-39M was essentially the same as the P-39L except that the V-1710-83 powerplant was installed. This engine, which had six exhaust stubs on each side and produced 1,360 horsepower, increased the top speed at 15,000 feet. A Curtiss Electric propeller was used on this variant. Eight P-39Ms had the two cameras added in the aft fuselage to become P-39M-2-BEs.

Easily the most numerous of the "mid-series" Airacobras was the P-39N, 2,095 of which were produced. In an effort to decrease weight, P-39Ns had a reduced internal fuel capacity of eighty-seven gallons, but kits were provided to the field to bring this back up to the standard 120 gallons where range was more important than the weight savings.

The first 500 N-models were P-39N-BEs, and they were powered by the V-1710-85 engine turning an Aeroproducts propeller with a diameter of 11' 4". The next 900 were designated P-39N-1-BEs, and they had an

A crew chief leans in through the left window to help his pilot as the engine on this P-39L is started on a cold winter day. Note the added vents on the nose which remained a production standard on all subsequent variants of the Airacobra. **(USAFM)**

Above: This Airacobra was assigned to a training unit within the United States. It was one of 240 P-39Ms produced. **(National Archives)**

Right: Although the .50-caliber machine guns have been removed, most details on the instrument panel in a P-39M are visible in this photograph. **(USAFM)**

P-39L 1/72nd SCALE DRAWING

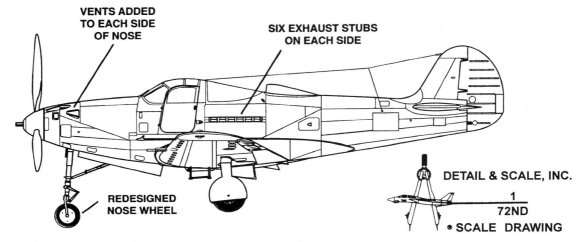

VENTS ADDED TO EACH SIDE OF NOSE

SIX EXHAUST STUBS ON EACH SIDE

REDESIGNED NOSE WHEEL

DETAIL & SCALE, INC.

1
72ND
SCALE DRAWING

DETAIL & SCALE, 1/72nd SCALE, COPYRIGHT © DRAWING BY LLOYD S. JONES

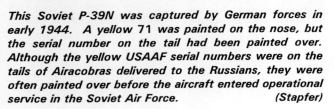

This Soviet P-39N was captured by German forces in early 1944. A yellow 71 was painted on the nose, but the serial number on the tail had been painted over. Although the yellow USAAF serial numbers were on the tails of Airacobras delivered to the Russians, they were often painted over before the aircraft entered operational service in the Soviet Air Force. *(Stapfer)*

Aeroproducts propeller with an increased diameter of 11' 7". The center of gravity was also adjusted in an attempt to reduce balance problems experienced when the heavy ammunition for the nose guns was expended. The final 695 were designated P-39N-5-BEs, and these had thirty-eight pounds of armor deleted. A small piece of armor was added in the rollover structure to protect the back of the pilot's head, replacing the clear bulletproof glass used on earlier variants. Two photographic reconnaissance conversions of the P-39N included 128 P-39N-2-BEs modified from P-39N-1-BEs and 35 P-39N-3-BEs converted from P-39N-BEs.

P-39Ns served extensively with the USAAF and the Soviet Air Force. Others were supplied to the Free French and the Italian Co-belligerent Forces after the Italian Armistice in May 1943.

DATA

Version	P-39N
Bell Model Number	26
Number Built	2,095
Armament	1 X 37-mm cannon, 2 x .50 caliber MG, 4 x .30 caliber MG
Powerplant	Allison V-1710-85
Horsepower	1,200
Maximum Speed	379 mph at 10,000 feet
Rate of Climb	3.8 minutes to 15,000 feet
Ceiling	38,500 feet
Maximum Range	1,250 miles
Combat Range	750 miles
Wingspan	34 feet
Length	30 feet, 2 inches
Height	12 feet, 5 inches
Empty Weight	5,675 pounds
Gross Weight	7,600 pounds
Maximum Take-off Weight	8,200 pounds
Maximum Internal Fuel	87 gallons*
Maximum External Fuel	175 gallons

* Kits could be added in the field to bring the internal fuel capacity back up to the usual 120 gallon capacity.

PHOTO RECONNAISSANCE CAMERA DETAILS

Above: A few Airacobras of most versions were converted to photographic reconnaissance aircraft with the addition of cameras. In each case, the camera arrangement was generally the same. The cameras were controlled by switches on a small panel located below and just aft of the throttle quadrant on the left side of the cockpit floor. (USAFM)

Right: This close-up shows the details on the camera control panel. (USAFM)

Below left: The two cameras were located in the lower aft fuselage just aft of the trailing edge of the wings. (USAFM)

Below right: With the covering panel removed, the two cameras are visible in their mount. (USAFM)

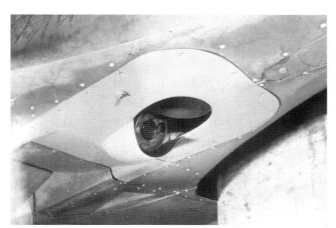

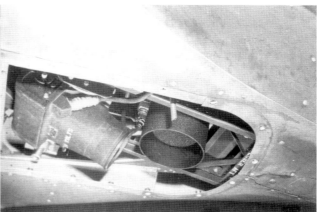

P-39Q

The P-39Q was the last production version of the Airacobra. The two .30-caliber machine guns in each wing were replaced by single .50-caliber weapons mounted in pods under each wing. These pods were removable and not always used in combat. **(National Archives)**

The final variant of the Airacobra was the P-39Q, and it was also the most numerous with no less than 4,905 being delivered in eight production blocks. Over half were exported to the Soviet Union, while others went to the Free French and Italian Co-belligerent Forces. The most noticeable difference between the P-39Q and the previous variant was the deletion of the .30-caliber machine guns in the wings. These were replaced with two detachable gun pods mounted under the wings, and each pod contained a single .50-caliber machine gun. Many P-39Qs, particularly those flown by the Russians,

were used operationally without these pods in place. Like the P-39N, the V-1710-85 engine, with six exhaust stubs on each side, was used to power the P-39Q.

The first production block was the P-39Q-1-BE, and these 150 Airacobras had the reduced internal fuel capacity of 87 gallons. As with the P-39N, kits were provided to the field to restore this to the standard 120 gallons. Five of the P-39Q-1-BEs were converted to photographic reconnaissance aircraft with the addition of cameras in the aft fuselage. These five Airacobras were redesignated P-39Q-2-BEs.

The next production block included 950 P-39Q-5-BEs in which the internal fuel capacity was increased to 110 gallons. Lighter armor was used to reduce weight. Two cameras were added to 148 P-39Q-5-BEs to create P-39Q-6-BEs.

P-39Q-10-BEs, of which 705 were delivered, had the full 120-gallon internal fuel capacity restored, and the

"Little HINX JINX II" was a P-39Q that operated from Port Morsby in late 1943. **(USAFM)**

P-39Qs operate from Makin in the Gilbert Islands during 1943. **(USAFM)**

Although this photograph is not of high quality, it is very rare and shows one of the P-39Q-25-BEs with the four-bladed propeller. Of all the Airacobras produced, only the P-39Q-21-BE and P-39Q-25-BE had four-bladed propellers, and almost all of them were delivered to the Russian Air Force. *(Stapfer)*

In addition to the two-seat trainers converted in the United States, the Soviets also modified several Airacobras to TP-39 trainers following the same concept established by Bell. No red star national insignias were applied to the upper surfaces of the wings, and this was often the case on Soviet aircraft. *(Stapfer)*

armor protection was increased. These Airacobras also had additional winterization protection. Automatic boost control was added, and the throttle and engine RPM controls were coordinated. Kits were made available to restore the engine control quadrant to separate operation if desired. Eight of these aircraft had cameras added to become P-39Q-11-BEs.

One thousand P-39Q-15-BEs were next off the production line, and these had only minor changes from the previous P-39Q-10-BE. The oxygen system was reduced from four bottles to only two.

The 891 P-39Q-20-BEs also had minor equipment changes. Those used by the USAAF and the Free French had the usual gun pods under the wings, but the ones delivered to the Russians did not have the pods.

Four-bladed Aeroproducts propellers were fitted to the 109 P-39Q-21-BEs, and the 700 P-39Q-25-BEs that followed. The large majority of these Airacobras were provided to the Soviet Union, and the gun pods were seldom, if ever, present. The P-39Q-25-BEs also had a reinforced aft fuselage and horizontal tail structure.

The final production block included 400 P-39Q-30-BEs, and for these Bell returned to the three-bladed propeller. When the last P-39Q-30-BE rolled off the assembly line, Airacobra production ended. By this time, Bell was already well into its delivery of P-63 Kingcobras and was working the P-59 Airacomet which was destined to become America's first operational jet fighter.

DATA

Version	P-39Q
Bell Model Number	26
Number Built	4,905
Armament	1 X 37-mm cannon, 4 x .50 caliber
Powerplant	Allison V-1710-85
Horsepower	1,200
Maximum Speed	385 mph at 15,000 feet
Rate of Climb	4.5 minutes to 15,000 feet
Ceiling	35,000 feet
Maximum Range	1,100 miles
Combat Range	650 miles
Wingspan	34 feet
Length	30 feet, 2 inches
Height	12 feet, 5 inches
Empty Weight	5,645 pounds
Gross Weight	7,700 pounds
Maximum Take-off Weight	8,350 pounds
Maximum Internal Fuel	120 gallons*
Maximum External Fuel	175 gallons

* The P-39Q-1-BE had a maximum internal fuel capacity of 87 gallons as delivered, but kits could be added in the field to bring the capacity back up to 120 gallons. The P-39A-5-BE had a maximum internal fuel capacity of 110 gallons.

The Soviets provided two Airacobras to Poland after World War II for evaluation purposes, but the Poles chose the Yak-9 as their standard postwar fighter. *(Stapfer)*

Two P-39Qs were transferred to the Navy for research and use as targets. They were given the Navy designation, F2L-1K. *(Jones collection)*

P-39Q DETAILS

The engine gage unit has been removed from the instrument panel in this P-39Q, but otherwise all of the features are illustrated. The aft ends of the two .50-caliber machine guns are clearly visible as well. *(USAFM)*

Details on the right side of the cockpit can be seen through the open left door. It appears that the control column in this aircraft has been painted flat black, although the paint is chipping badly. *(USAFM)*

A close-up shows details of the throttle quadrant. Just forward of it is the auxiliary fuse box. The ammeter and electrical switches are located on the vertical panel at the extreme left side of the cockpit. *(USAFM)*

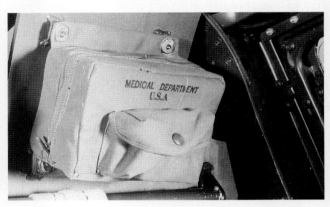

The first aid kit was moved to a position on the head armor behind the pilot on the P-39Q-15-BE. On earlier Airacobras, it had been located on the left cabin door. *(USAFM)*

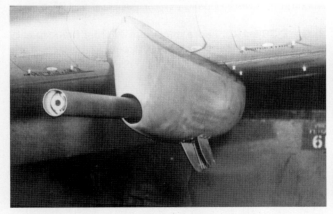

A close-up provides a good look at the .50-caliber machine gun pod which replaced the two .30-caliber weapons on the P-39Q. But these pods were sometimes deleted, leaving the Airacobra to rely entirely on the weapons in its nose. A chute for the spent shells can be seen beneath the pod. These guns had to be charged manually on the ground before take off. *(USAFM)*

Because of their short range, Airacobras were often seen with fuel tanks on their centerline stations. The most common size was this 75-gallon tank that was quite aerodynamic and therefore offered little drag. It was built by the Alcoa Aluminum Company and was attached to a standard bomb rack. Anti-sway braces on each side of the tank held it steady in the airstream. *(USAFM)*

P-39Qs from the 362nd Fighter Squadron of the 357th Fighter Group are parked on the ramp at Hayward Field, California, in 1943. (Olmstead via Roeder)

A P-39Q waits to have its guns boresighted on a firing range. (National Archives)

These P-39Qs were painted in white Zebra stripes and used for training in the United States. They often played the role of the enemy and flew mock attacks against fledgling fighter pilots and gunners in bomber aircraft. (USAFM)

TP-39 1/72nd SCALE DRAWING

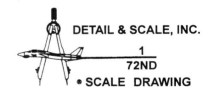

DETAIL & SCALE, INC.

$$\frac{1}{72ND}$$

* SCALE DRAWING

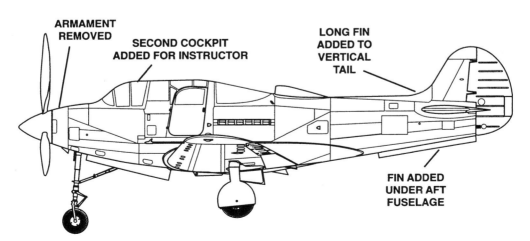

ARMAMENT REMOVED

SECOND COCKPIT ADDED FOR INSTRUCTOR

LONG FIN ADDED TO VERTICAL TAIL

FIN ADDED UNDER AFT FUSELAGE

DETAIL & SCALE, 1/72nd SCALE, COPYRIGHT © DRAWING BY LLOYD S. JONES

P-39Q, 1/72nd SCALE, FIVE-VIEW DRAWINGS

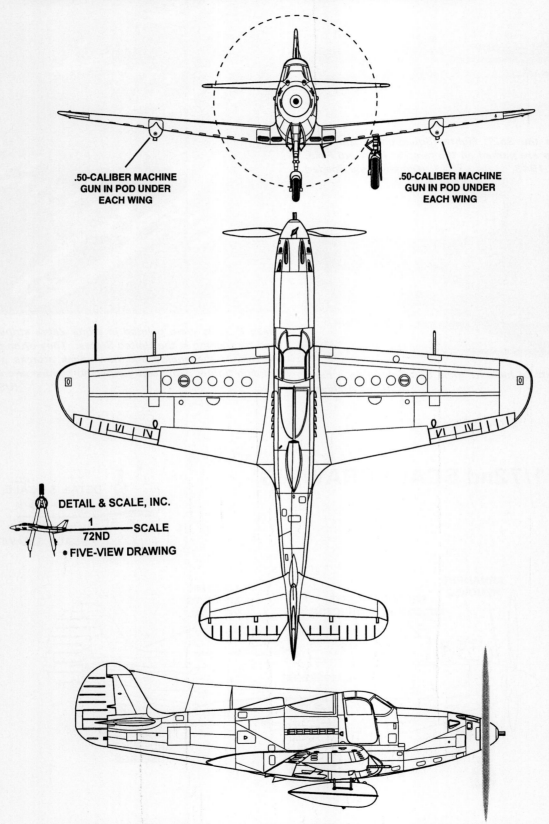

.50-CALIBER MACHINE GUN IN POD UNDER EACH WING

.50-CALIBER MACHINE GUN IN POD UNDER EACH WING

DETAIL & SCALE, INC.

$\dfrac{1}{72\text{ND}}$ SCALE

• FIVE-VIEW DRAWING

DETAIL & SCALE, 1/72nd SCALE, COPYRIGHT © DRAWINGS BY LLOYD S. JONES

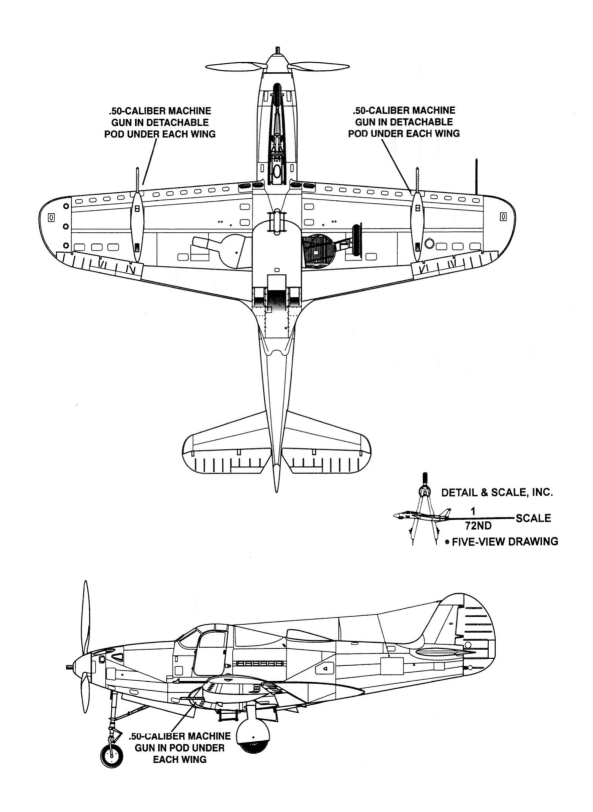

.50-CALIBER MACHINE
GUN IN DETACHABLE
POD UNDER EACH WING

.50-CALIBER MACHINE
GUN IN DETACHABLE
POD UNDER EACH WING

DETAIL & SCALE, INC.

$\dfrac{1}{72\text{ND}}$ ── SCALE

• FIVE-VIEW DRAWING

.50-CALIBER MACHINE
GUN IN POD UNDER
EACH WING

DETAIL & SCALE, 1/72nd SCALE, COPYRIGHT © DRAWINGS BY LLOYD S. JONES

XP-39E

Three XP-39Es were built to test different wing, tail, and rudder designs and combinations. Some sources state that the laminar flow wing design, used later on the P-63, was also used on these aircraft, but photographs indicate that this was not the case. However, much information and data gathered from the three XP-39Es was applied to the development of the P-63, and two of the XP-39Es were later converted to XP-63s as shown on page 56. Although original plans called for these Airacobras to be powered by the Continental V-1430 powerplant, the Allison V-1710-47 was installed instead. It had a two-stage supercharger, and it turned an Aeroproducts propeller. To accommodate the supercharger, the aft fuselage was lengthened 21.3 inches. A planned production version of this design, designated the P-76, was canceled. (Above and left, National Archives, below, Jones collection)

COLOR GALLERY

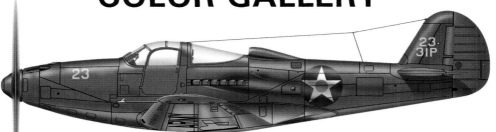

Most of the twenty P-39Cs were assigned to the 31st Pursuit Group. They were the first Airacobras painted in the standard Olive Drab over Neutral Gray camouflage scheme, and they had simple pre-war markings.

This P-400 was flown by Lt. Zed Fountain of the 347th Fighter Group in New Caledonia during April and May 1942. It was painted in British Earth Brown and Dark Green camouflage, and it retained its RAF serial, BW146.

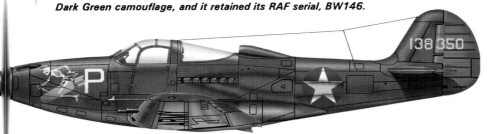

Flown by Lt. I. A. Erickson, this P-39D-1-BE was assigned to the 35th Fighter Squadron of the 8th Fighter Group. The unit operated from Milne Bay, New Guinea, in 1942.

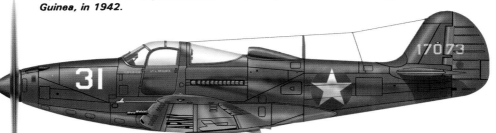

Lt. Leslie Spoonts flew this P-39J while he was assigned to the 57th Fighter Squadron of the 54th Fighter Group. The 54th FG was stationed in Alaska from June through December 1942, and it operated in the Aleutians.

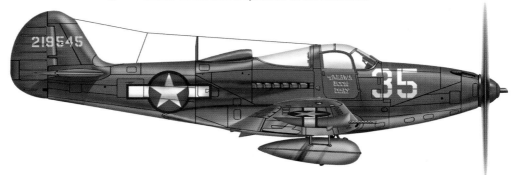

"TARAWA BOOM DEAY" was a P-39Q-1-BE flown by Major Joseph H. Powell. He served with the 72nd Fighter Squadron of the 21st Fighter Group in the Mariana Islands during 1944.

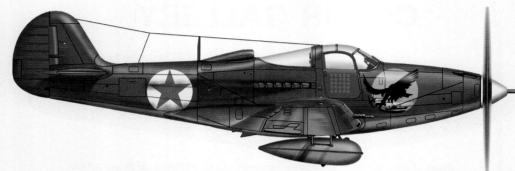

This P-39N was flown by Major V. F. Sirotin of the Soviet Air Force in 1944.

Kingcobras delivered to the Soviet Air Force were painted in the standard USAAF scheme of Olive Drab over Neutral Gray. Yellow USAAF serials were usually retained.

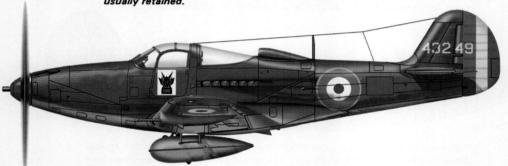

The Free French flew this P-39Q during 1944 as part of GC III/6 "Roussillon." This French unit flew patrols along the coast of Africa.

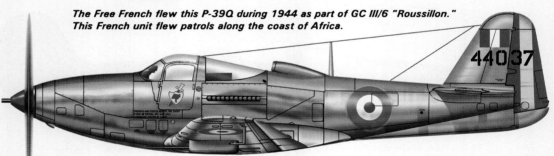

This P-63C Kingcobra was flown by GC II/9 "Auvergne" in Indochina during 1949.

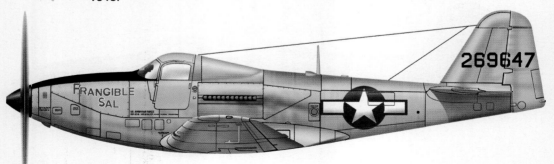

"FRANGIBLE SAL" was an RP-63A used as a target aircraft to train USAAF bomber crewmen in the art of aerial gunnery.

P-39 AIRACOBRA COLORS

Above: A test pilot finishes his cockpit checks before starting the engine on one of the thirteen YP-39 proto-types. Note the fairings over the machine gun ports on top of the nose, although no armament appears to be present on this aircraft. *(Piet collection)*

Right: Wearing typical flying clothes of the day, a test pilot poses with one of the YP-39s. Note the markings on the natural metal Curtiss Electric propeller. *(Piet collection)*

Below: A P-39C shares the ramp with one of the YP-39s as flight tests are conducted with the Airacobra. Note that the natural metal YP-39 has the 37-mm cannon installed, while the P-39C does not. *(Piet collection)*

Above: Most of the twenty P-39Cs were flown by the 31st Pursuit Group as service test aircraft. The aircraft are painted in the standard USAAC Olive Drab over Neutral Gray scheme. (Piet collection)

Left: The British initially chose this Earth Brown and Dark Green camouflage for its Airacobra Is, but photographic evidence indicates that a few were painted in a gray and green camouflage scheme. (Piet collection)

Below: P-39Ds of the 8th Pursuit Group carry red crosses to indicate that they were part of the red force during the Carolina Maneuvers in 1941. Other sources have misidentified these 8th Pursuit Group's Airacobras as P-39Cs, but they were P-39Ds instead. (Piet collection)

Above: Ground crew personnel from the 54th Fighter Group labor inside the engine compartment and on the nose and wing armament to get a well worn P-39F ready for another mission against the Japanese in the Aleutian Islands. *(Piet collection)*

Right: An armorer loads 37-mm cannon ammunition into the weapon's magazine. *(Piet collection)*

Below: Laboring under the protection of a wooden frame shelter, maintenance personnel work on a P-39Q in the Canal Zone. Note the unmarked and unpainted propeller on this Airacobra. *(Piet collection)*

P-39N COCKPIT DETAILS & COLORS

The Yanks Air Museum in Chino, California, is meticulously restoring a P-39N to original condition. Note the aft end of the .50-caliber machine guns with their red charging handles.

A special green paint was used by Bell in the cockpit interiors of P-39s and P-63s. All colors shown here are to factory specifications. Note how the throttle quadrant is mounted on the left door jam.

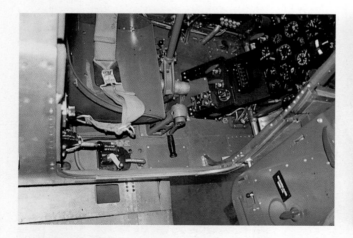

There were no side consoles in the Airacobra. Instead, items were mounted on the floor to each side of the seat. The handle located low on the turnover structure is the oil shutter control. The silver handle on the black housing on the floor is the coolant shutter control, while the handle just forward of it is the landing gear control handle. The crank at the corner of the seat is the landing gear emergency control crank.

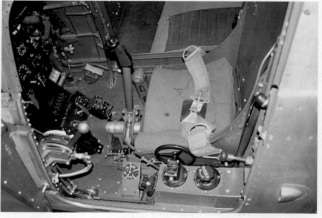

The large black wheel to the left of the seat is the elevator trim tab control. It is mounted into the black housing on top of the small rectangular box between the seat and the door. The control knob for the trim tab on the rudder is also on top of the box, while the aileron trim tab is on the front of the box. The fuel selector switch is located near the front left corner of the seat, and the bomb arm and safe lever is to the left of the control column.

Above, left and right: The interior surfaces of the doors were painted the Bell green color. Since it would be difficult to open the door against the airstream if the pilot needed to bail out, both doors could be jettisoned from their hinges to allow easy egress from the cockpit while the aircraft was in flight. The data and map case was mounted on the right door, and placards explaining the landing gear and flap operations were affixed to it.

The decking behind the seat and rollover structure was often used to mount radio gear. The particular radios used sometimes varied from one version of the Airacobra to the next, and different radios were used depending on where the aircraft was operating. The right side of the rear canopy glass was hinged to open along the centerline to provide easy access to the equipment on the deck.

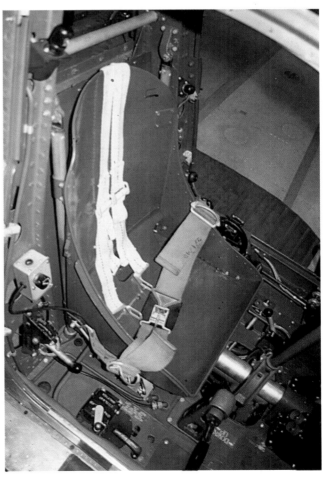

Details of the metal seat, lap belts, and shoulder harnesses are visible in this view from the right side.

AIRACOBRA NOSE DETAILS & COLORS

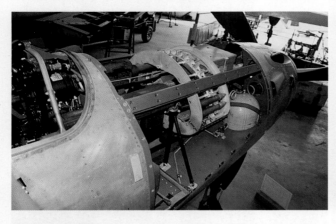

The six photographs on this page show the nose compartment in the Yanks Air Museum's P-39N during restoration. With the two .50-caliber ammunition boxes removed, much of the inner structure is also visible.

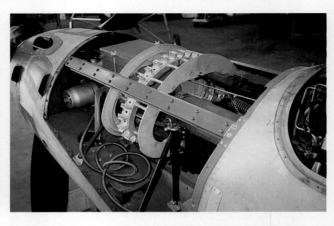

Details of the magazine for the 37-mm cannon ammunition are visible here. Note how the two .50-caliber machine guns are mounted just under the structure of the magazine.

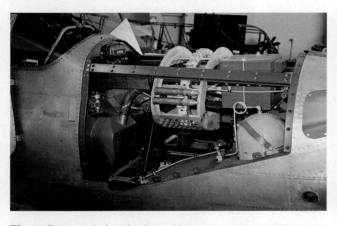

The yellow tank for the breathing oxygen is visible in this right side view. The battery box would have been flat black on operational aircraft rather than a light red as shown here. The interior of the nose compartment was painted the same Bell green color as the inside of the cockpit.

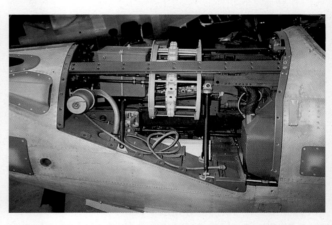

An unobstructed view from the left side shows the cannon mounted at the center of the compartment and the two machine guns above it. The horizontal frame, to which the panels were fastened, got in the way of armorers and maintenance personnel, so the panels were redesigned on the P-63 Kingcobra.

The oil tank for the gear box was mounted forward of the battery box in the very front of the compartment.

At the aft end of the compartment was the small expansion tank for the brake fluid.

P-39 LANDING GEAR DETAILS & COLORS
NOSE LANDING GEAR

The nose gear was both simple and very sturdy. A small door was attached to the top of the strut to cover the forward end of the well, while two longer doors were mounted along the sides of the well. The gear struts, interior of the nose gear well, and the inside surfaces of the gear doors were painted the Bell green color as a standard. However, color photographs taken in the field provide evidence that a steel color was also used on the struts, particularly on early versions of the Airacobra.

A close-up provides a good look at the nose wheel, tire, fork, and link. Early P-39s had a smaller wheel with a bigger tire than the design shown here, but this design was more aerodynamic, and it became standard beginning with the P-39L.

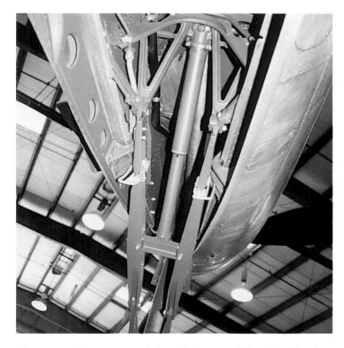

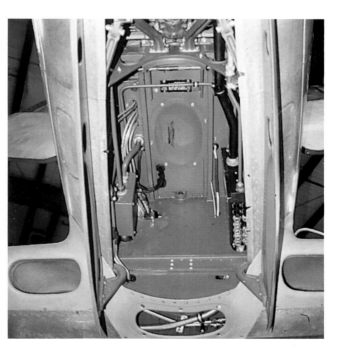

The retraction strut and drag link are evident in this view that looks forward into the nose gear well. The drive shaft between the engine and the gear box can also be seen in the front half of the well.

The wheel and tire fit up into the aft end of the gear well. A small bulge is evident in the top of the well to provide sufficient clearance for the tire. Also note the hinges for the doors in this photo and the one to the left.

LEFT LANDING GEAR

Above left: An inside view of the left main landing gear shows the silver colored wheel and the Bell green color used on the struts and doors. Also note the hydraulic line for the brakes just aft of the strut.

Above right: The alignment of the two outer gear doors and the strut is apparent from directly in front of the gear. Notice how the upper and lower gear doors overlapped slightly to allow for extension and contraction of the oleo.

Below left: The outer portion of the gear well housed the strut when the gear was retracted. Note the Bell green color inside the well except where the strut is attached. That outer part of the well is Chromate Yellow Primer.

Below right: The inner part of each main gear well had ribbing at the top, and a small door was hinged along its edge. The door closed over the gear when the retracting tire pushed against the tab near the center of the rod between the door and the well.

RIGHT LANDING GEAR

Above left: Details on the inside of the right main gear are evident here. The right gear was simply a mirror image of the left.

Above right: A rear view of the right main gear shows how the hydraulic brake line extended down from inside the well, along the strut, and then connected to the inside of the wheel. Also note how the lower door was attached to the strut.

Below left: The inner wall of each main gear well had a large cutout area to allow sufficient clearance for the retracted wheel and tire. There was also a slightly indented area in the ducting just beyond the cutout.

Below right: The Bell green color was painted inside most of the outer section of the main gear wells, but here again, the Chromate Yellow Primer can be seen in the area where the strut was attached to the wing assembly.

ALLISON V-1710 DETAILS & COLORS

Different versions of the Allison V-1710 engine powered all variants of the P-39 Airacobra as well as the P-63 Kingcobra. This V-1710 is one that has the twelve fishtail exhaust ports on each side. Note the lack of a gear case on the front side. Instead, a long shaft extends forward from the block.

The shaft extended forward to the housing for the reduction gears that was located just aft of the propeller hub. This view shows how the cannon was mounted through the housing and propeller hub.

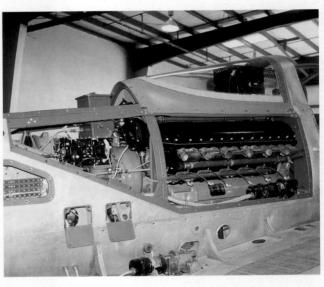

Details on the rear of the V-1710 are shown here from the right side.

The installed engine could be serviced through two removable panels on each side of the fuselage and another panel on the spine just aft of the rear canopy glass.

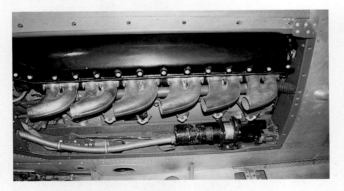

Engines with the six exhaust stubs on each side actually had the same twelve outlets coming out of the cylinders, but they were channeled in pairs into the six stubs. Note that the ends of the stubs have a circular cross section rather than being flattened to the fishtail configuration.

The left access panels have been removed from this P-39N Airacobra to reveal the engine from the left side.

KINGCOBRA NOSE DETAILS & COLORS

The access panels covering the Kingcobra's gun compartment were redesigned to provide easier access to the guns and other equipment inside. Note the lack of any horizontal framework as found on the P-39 Airacobra.

In restoring Frank Borman's P-63A, Square One Aviation in Chino, California, did an incredible job in the nose compartment to include the cannon and two machine guns. Each 37-mm cannon shell was turned out of brass, then painted and marked accurately. Also note the stenciling inside the compartment.

Tanks for breathing oxygen were located on both sides of the compartment near the forward end. Although the cannon and machine guns were located and mounted in much the same way as they were in the Airacobra, the other items inside the compartment were rearranged and redesigned to some extent.

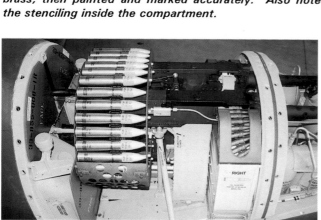

The inside of the compartment was painted Chromate Yellow Primer. Note the location of the ammunition boxes for the two .50-caliber machine guns. The right gun was fed with ammunition from the right, while the left gun was fed from the left.

The oil tank for the gear box was also redesigned, and it was more easily accessible than the one in the P-39.

KINGCOBRA COCKPIT DETAILS & COLORS

A closer view of the instrument panel shows some differences in the details when compared to the P-39N. There are considerable variations in the arrangement of the instruments, and there are no manual charging handles for the machine guns.

An overall view of the cockpit in the Kingcobra at the Yanks Air Museum reveals a lot of similarities with the P-39N shown on page 38. Again, the Bell green color is used for the cockpit's interior.

The items on the left side of the cockpit were essentially the same as those in the P-39. They include the trim control wheel and knobs, the fuel selector switch, and the bomb arm and safe lever.

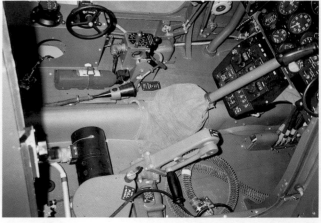

This photo, along with the middle and lower photographs to the right, was taken in the magnificently restored P-63A owned by former astronaut, Frank Borman. Details of the seat are illustrated here, and it is apparent that it is quite different from the one used in the P-39.

With the seat removed, additional details on the floor of the cockpit are visible. These include a fire extinguisher and the relief tube. Also note the canvas area at the base of the control column.

Above, left and right: The inside surfaces of the P-63A's two cockpit doors had the red handles like those in the P-39. The smaller red handles raised and lowered the windows. The map case was located on the inside of the right door. All four photographs on this page were taken in Frank Borman's P-63A.

Below left: A view through the rear glass of the cockpit enclosure shows details of the radio receiver on the rear deck.

Below right: With the seat removed, the armor behind the pilot is visible as is the first aid kit mounted at the top.

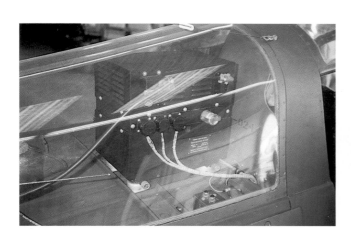

P-63 KINGCOBRA COLORS

Above: A rare color photograph of Russian P-63As shows the USAAF standard Olive Drab over Neutral Gray paint scheme and yellow U. S. serial number. Many Russian P-39s and P-63s had a white disc painted around the red star insignia. (Piet collection)

Left: Several P-63s were used for racing after the war. The most extensively modified was converted by Pylon-Air and flown by Larry Havens. It had artwork for Crazy Horse Campgrounds on the nose. (Jones)

Below: Looking much more like a standard Kingcobra, number N62822 was painted in a brilliant red finish and flown at the Reno Air Races by John Sandburg. (Jones)

P-39 AIRACOBRA DETAILS
COCKPIT ENCLOSURE DETAILS

Above, an overall view from the left side shows the entire cockpit enclosure which remained virtually unchanged throughout all Airacobra production. In spite of the rather large framework, visibility from the cockpit was considered to be quite good.

Right: A small "clear view panel" could be opened on the left side of the windscreen to provide a clear forward view in the event the windscreen became covered with sleet, ice, or oil.

The windows in the doors could be rolled down, and this helped keep the cockpit cool in hot areas. But the doors also leaked air, and in colder climates the left door was often taped along its edges to make it airtight. Pilots usually used the right door to enter and exit the cockpit.

Radio gear can be seen through the aft section of the cockpit enclosure in this P-39Q. Compare the equipment seen here with the single unit shown on page 39. Notice also how the wire for the radio antenna is attached to the rollover structure.

FUSELAGE DETAILS

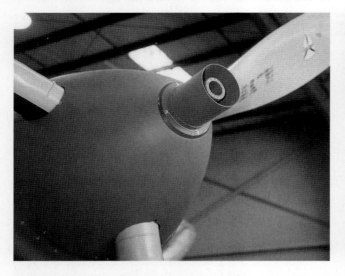

The 37-mm cannon barrel was often protected by a tube around it. The longer 20-mm cannon barrel was left unprotected.

The forward fuselage tapered smoothly into the spinner. Small pieces of the spinner fit behind each blade of the propeller to form a tight fit.

Beginning with the P-39L, a second and larger vent was added to each side of the nose. Also notice the hoist hole that extends through the nose below the vent.

Vents on the left side of the nose are shown here along with the depression for the left .50-caliber machine gun. A small metal cover protected the muzzle of the weapon.

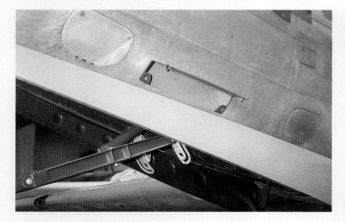

A chute on each side of the nose held the .50-caliber shells after they were fired. The door covering the chute could be opened as shown here to remove the shells after the aircraft returned from its mission. The interior of the chute was painted with Chromate Yellow Primer.

The data block on the Airacobra was stenciled just forward of and below the door on the left side.

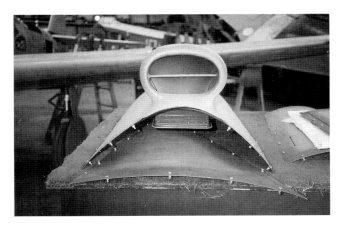

A front view looks directly into the scoop for the carburetion air that was mounted behind the cockpit. Note the airflow divider running horizontally across the inside of the scoop. The boxlike structure beneath the scoop fit on to the duct seen in the photo at right.

The panel and scoop shown at left covered this part of the aft fuselage. At the forward end was the duct leading to the carburetor. The silver engine oil tank can be seen further aft, and the antenna mast is also visible. It was made out of wood and painted to match the exterior of the aircraft.

The flaps were operated by an electric motor located under the fairing at the base of the right wing root.

This plumbing was under the fairing for the left wing root, and it included the link that operated the left flap.

Radio equipment was also mounted in the aft fuselage compartment. It can be seen here through an open access panel on the left side of the aircraft.

A hoist tube ran all the way through the aft fuselage. The white insulator on the spine is where the antenna wire for the radio shown at left entered the aircraft.

WING DETAILS

Above, left and right: Inlets in the leading edge of each wing root provided air to the two oil coolers and the radiator for the engine coolant.

Left: The split flaps were simple in design, and they were operated electrically. This photograph shows the flap for the left wing of the P-39N being restored at the Yanks Air Museum in Chino, California.

Below, left and right: The ailerons were covered with fabric, and each had trim and balance tabs extending outward from the inboard edge.

Above, left and right: Stainless steel blast tubes covered the barrels of the .30-caliber machine guns that were mounted in the wings of all Airacobra variants between the P-39D and P-39N. Spent shells and links were jettisoned through four slots under the wing as shown in the photograph at right. These two photographs show the blast tubes and slots on the left wing.

Right: A standard pitot probe, like that used on many other U. S. aircraft during World War II, was fitted on the leading edge of the left wing near the tip.

Below left: With the panels removed, the plumbing and other items in the lower fuselage are visible between the two inner landing gear doors. The radiators for the oil coolers and engine coolant were located in this area.

Below right: A standard bomb rack was mounted on the centerline underneath the fuselage. An external fuel tank or a bomb up to the 500-pound size could be carried on this rack.

A fuel filler for the wing tanks was located on top of each wing. It was usually painted red.

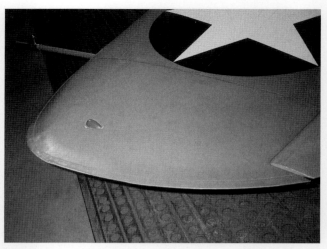

Navigation lights were on the top and bottom of each wing tip panel. This is the red light on top of the left wing tip.

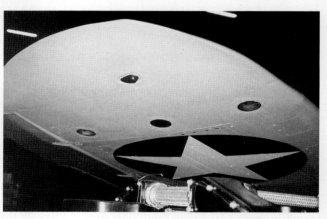

The green navigation light on the bottom of the right wing is shown here along with the three identification lights which were only under the right wing tip. They were red, blue-green, and amber from front to rear.

The red navigation light under the left wing tip is visible here as is the retractable landing/taxi light. Also note the three hinges on the aileron.

The retractable landing/taxi light was under the left wing just aft of the slots for the wing guns.

TAIL DETAILS

Above: The vertical stabilizer had an area of 7.9 square feet, and it was offset one degree to the left to counter the torque of the engine. Its chord was 43.875 inches, and it was 44.52 inches high. A white navigation light was located about half way up the trailing edge on each side, and it can be seen just inside the 7 in the tail number on this aircraft.

Left: The rudder was covered with fabric, and it had a total area of 11.07 square feet to include the balance area. Movement of the rudder was thirty degrees left and right. The trim tab on the rudder was .37 square feet, and it had a movement of twenty degrees left and right.

Like the ailerons and rudder, the elevators were covered with fabric. Both elevators combined for a total of 16.22 square feet, and they could be moved thirty-five degrees up and fifteen degrees down. The trim tab on the left elevator had an area of .86 square feet and a movement of twenty degrees up and down. The horizontal stabilizers had a total of 23.9 square feet, and they were set at an angle of 2.25 degrees to the longitudinal axis. Their chord, including the elevator, was 52.25 inches, and they had a span of 13 feet.

P-63 KINGCOBRA VARIANTS
XP-63 & XP-63A

Above: Two of the XP-39Es, 41-19511 and 41-19512, were converted to XP-63 prototypes. Each was fitted with laminar flow wings, a V-1710-47 engine with six exhaust stubs on each side, and a four-blade propeller. Bell's chief test pilot, Robert M. Stanley, made the initial flight in the first XP-63 on December 7, 1942, and the second XP-63 first flew on March 4, 1943, but both aircraft were destroyed in crashes. (National Archives)

Below: One XP-63A, 42-78015, was also built, and it differed from the XP-63s in that it was powered by a V-1710-93 engine with twelve exhaust stubs on each side. Top speed was 426 miles per hour, and this put the XP-63A in the same speed class as the best fighters of the day. Provisions were also included for underwing racks which could carry bombs or external fuel tanks. (Jones collection)

P-63A

The first production version of the Kingcobra was the P-63A. A total of 1,725 were built, and these were divided among seven production blocks. Beginning with the P-63A-6-BE, underwing racks were added to carry 500-pound bombs or external fuel tanks as shown here.
(USAFM)

The first production version of the Kingcobra was the P-63A, and there were seven different production blocks covering the 1,725 aircraft. All were powered by the Allison V-1710-95 engine with a two-stage supercharger mounted behind the powerplant. The horizontal tail area was increased over what was used on the XP-63, and on the aircraft in the -1, -5, -6, and -7 production blocks, the propeller diameter was 11' 7", one inch larger than the one used on the XP-63. The P-63A-1-BE, of which fifty were delivered, had an M4 37-mm cannon with thirty rounds. The two nose-mounted .50-caliber ma-

chine guns were supplied with 270 rounds each, and 250 rounds were carried for the two pod-mounted .50-caliber guns under the wings.

Only twenty P-63A-5-BEs were completed, and these had additional armor protection and different radios than used in the earlier P-63A-1-BEs. They were delivered to the Soviet Union without .50-caliber machine gun pods under the wings.

Beginning with the P-63A-6-BE, underwing racks were added to carry external fuel tanks up to the 75-gallon size and bombs up to the 500-pound class. These were in addition to the centerline rack that was standard on the earlier blocks. A total of 130 P-63A-6-BEs were produced, and these were followed by 150 P-63A-7-BEs. Beginning with the -7 production block, aircraft delivered to the USAAF were left in a natural metal finish, while those provided to the Soviet Union remained in the Olive Drab over Neutral Gray paint scheme. The span of the horizontal tail was increased by sixteen inches, and the

Like the P-39Q Airacobra, Kingcobras could be fitted with a pod containing a .50-caliber machine gun under each wing. The pod was a different design than the one used on the P-39Q. The air inlets for the radiators for the oil coolers and the engine coolant were also redesigned. There was one large inlet in each wing root on the Kingcobra instead of the two smaller inlets in each root as found on the Airacobra. *(USAFM)*

The P-63A did not have the fin under the tail section that would appear later on the P-63C. Also note that the pitot probe was changed from the straight design on the leading edge of the left wing to an L-shaped design under the wing. On some Kingcobras, the two sections of the L were at ninety degrees to each other, but on most, the vertical section of the probe was angled back slightly. *(USAFM)*

The fifth P-63A-1-BE is shown here during a service evaluation flight. Early production P-63As were painted in the Olive Drab over Neutral Gray paint scheme.
(National Archives)

orange color to increase visibility. The five RP-63A-11-BEs were followed by ninety-five similar RP-63A-12-BEs that were produced from Kingcobras originally ordered in the P-63A-10-BE production block.

elevator chord was increased by two inches.

Water injection was initially added on the 200 P-63A-8-BEs, and the propeller was changed to a new Aeroproducts design with an eleven-foot diameter. The P-63A-9-BEs were the same as the previous P-63A-8-BEs except that additional armor was added to protect the pilot.

The final production block was the P-63A-10-BE, and 730 were produced, primarily for the Soviet Union. The M4 37-mm cannon was replaced with an M10 weapon of the same caliber, and the amount of ammunition for it was increased from thirty to fifty-eight rounds. The gun sight was changed to the N-9 electrical sight.

The first of the Kingcobras used as manned target aircraft in the USAAF came from the P-63A-9-BE production block. Five were converted to RP-63A-11-BEs with the addition of a thicker skin, revised armor, and a redundant pitot system. All armament was removed as was the water injection system and provisions for carrying external fuel tanks. They were painted a bright yellow-

DATA

Version	P-63A
Number Built	1,725
Armament	1 X 37-mm cannon, 4 x .50 caliber
Powerplant	Allison V-1710-93 or -95
Horsepower	1,325
Maximum Speed	410 mph at 25,000 feet
Rate of Climb	7.3 minutes to 25,000 feet
Ceiling	43,000 feet
Maximum Range	2,200 miles
Combat Range	450 miles
Wingspan	38 feet, 4 inches
Length	32 feet, 8 inches
Height	10 feet, 6.25 inches
Empty Weight	6,375 pounds
Gross Weight	8,800 pounds
Maximum Take-off Weight	10,500 pounds
Maximum Internal Fuel	126 gallons
Maximum External Fuel	325 gallons

Most P-63As and subsequent versions of the Kingcobra used by the USAAF in the fighter training role were delivered in a natural metal finish. A direct side view of a P-63A-9-BE shows the pitot probe that was angled back slightly under the left wing. *(USAFM)*

Kingcobras never saw combat with the USAAF, but they did serve as advanced trainers. These aircraft usually did not have their 37-mm cannon installed, and many had no armament at all. Yellow noses and large black training numbers are painted on these P-63A-7-BEs. *(USAFM)*

Above and right: Many Kingcobras, like this P-63A-10-BE, were delivered to the Soviet Union, and they were used extensively in combat in the ground attack role. They were delivered in the standard USAAF Olive Drab over Neutral Gray paint scheme with yellow U. S. serials on their vertical tails. Although most had white discs painted around each red star insignia, on some aircraft the red stars were simply outlined with white as shown here. Underwing tanks were usually painted silver or were natural metal. Also note the loop antenna on the spine of the aircraft.

(Both, Roeder collection)

P-63As, destined for delivery to the Soviet Union near completion at the Bell plant. These aircraft have the white disc painted around the red stars. This photograph also provides proof that the attachment for the external starter crank was added to the tube around the 37-mm cannon at the factory rather than in the field.

(Roeder collection)

Because their tail sections have not yet been installed, tail numbers have been hand written in crayon on the nose sections so that workers can keep track of these P-63A-10-BEs at the Bell factory. They are almost ready for the ferry pilots who will fly them to Alaska where they will be turned over to Russian pilots.

(Roeder collection)

RP-63A

Five P-63A-9-BEs were converted to RP-63A-11-BE target aircraft, and these were followed by ninety-five more conversions that were designated RP-63A-12-BEs. All armament and standard armor was deleted, and a thicker skin and non-standard armor protection was added to protect the aircraft and pilot from frangible bullets fired from crewmen in bombers as they developed the skills necessary to protect their aircraft with defensive machine guns. RP-63A-11-BE, 42-69654, was originally completed with a bright yellow-orange finish and a flat black IL76 on its nose. Note that the standard carburetor intake scoop has been removed and replaced with a smaller retractable scoop. There is protection above the exhaust stubs, and the glazing above the rear decking has been replaced with metal skin. In 1948, RP-63As that remained in the inventory were redesignated QF-63A-BEs. (USAFM)

The same aircraft in the top photo is shown again with the name "PIN BALL" on each side of the nose, but it still has the overall yellow-orange finish. Note the second pitot probe under the right wing in case the standard one under the left wing was damaged. (National Archives)

RP-63A-11-BE, 42-69654, is shown once again, but now it has a natural metal finish. The name "PIN BALL" was generally applied to all Kingcobra aircraft, because they had lights that flashed when hits were scored by the gunners in the bombers. (National Archives.

RP-63A-11-BE, 42-69647, was another target aircraft named "FRANGIBLE SAL" to reflect the type of bullets fired at it. These bullets turned to dust on impact on the plane, and they usually caused no damage. A color profile of this Kingcobra appears on page 34. (USAFM)

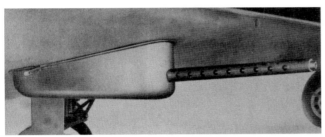

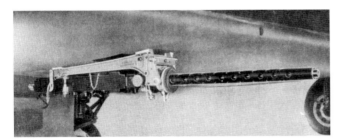

Above left: When they were carried, the .50-caliber machine gun pods were mounted inboard of the pylons under each wing of the Kingcobra. (USAFM)

Above right: An official USAAF photograph illustrates the features on the instrument panel in a P-63A. (USAFM)

Middle left: The gun pods carried under the wings of the Kingcobra were more streamlined and not as deep as the ones used on the P-39Q Airacobra. (USAFM)

Lower left: With the cover on the pod removed, the supporting structure and details of the .50-caliber machine gun are revealed. (USAFM)

RP-63A-12-BE 1/72nd SCALE DRAWING

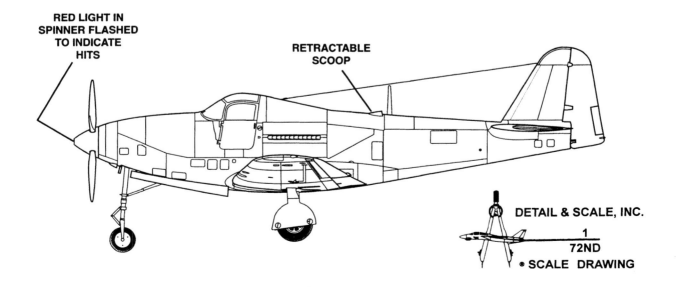

RED LIGHT IN SPINNER FLASHED TO INDICATE HITS

RETRACTABLE SCOOP

DETAIL & SCALE, INC.

1
72ND
● SCALE DRAWING

DETAIL & SCALE, 1/72nd SCALE, COPYRIGHT © DRAWING BY LLOYD S. JONES

P-63A, 1/72nd SCALE, MULTI-VIEW DRAWINGS

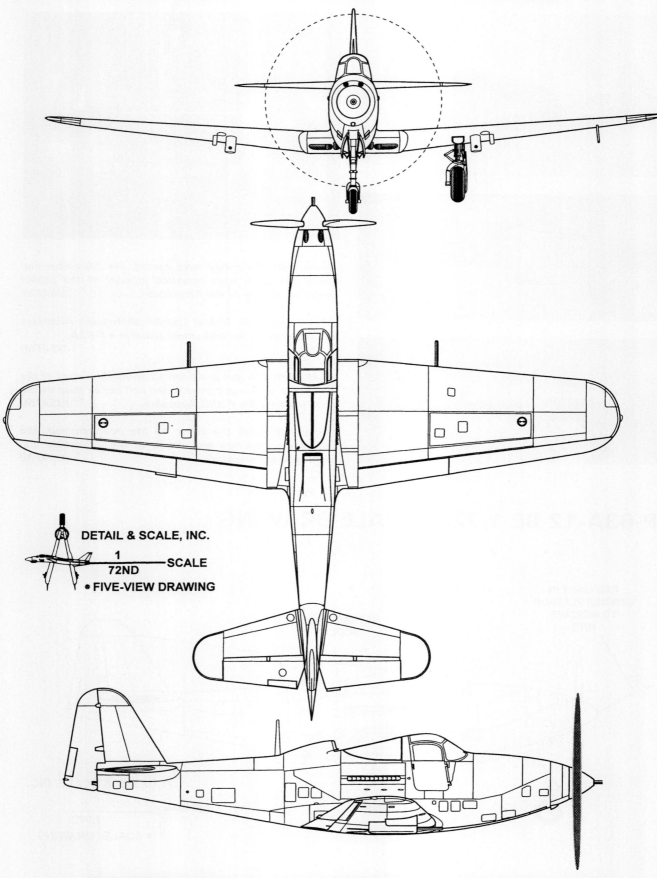

DETAIL & SCALE, INC.

$\dfrac{1}{72\text{ND}}$ —— SCALE

● FIVE-VIEW DRAWING

DETAIL & SCALE, 1/72nd SCALE, COPYRIGHT © DRAWINGS BY LLOYD S. JONES

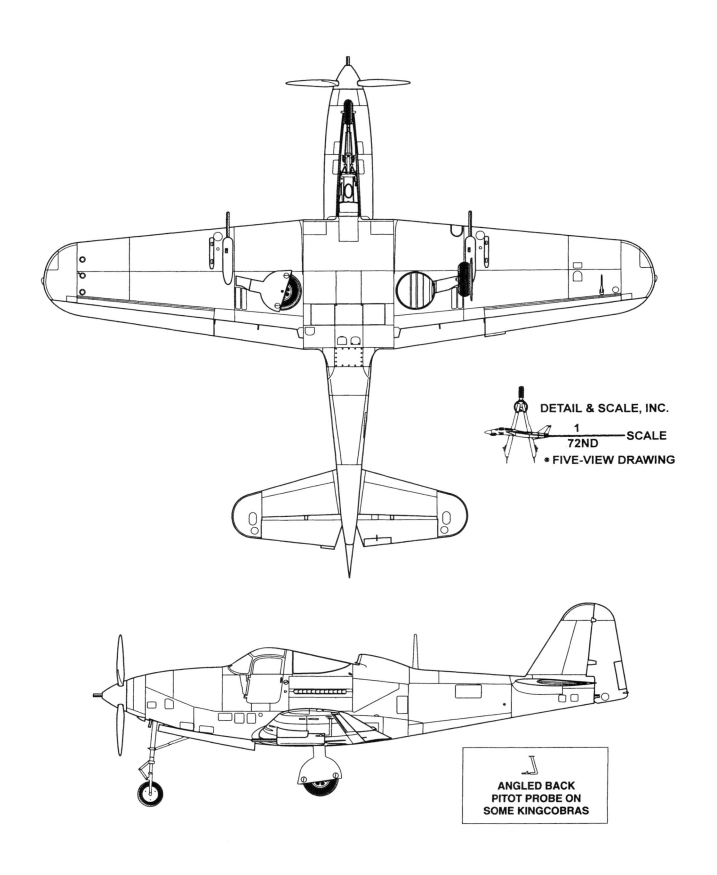

DETAIL & SCALE, INC.

$$\frac{1}{72ND}$$ SCALE

• FIVE-VIEW DRAWING

ANGLED BACK
PITOT PROBE ON
SOME KINGCOBRAS

DETAIL & SCALE, 1/72nd SCALE, COPYRIGHT © DRAWINGS BY LLOYD S. JONES

P-63C

A P-63C-5-RE is prepared for its ferry flight to the Soviet Union. The large strake under the aft fuselage, which first appeared on this version of the Kingcobra, is clearly visible in this side view. **(Roeder collection)**

The second and final production version of the Kingcobra to be delivered in quantity was the P-63C. A total of 1,227 were divided between two production blocks, but there were only very minor differences between the two. First off the production line were 215 P-63C-1-BEs, and these were followed by 1,012 P-63C-5-BEs. All P-63Cs were powered by the Allison V-1710-117 engine, and they could be identified from the earlier P-63As by the addition of a long ventral fin under the aft fuselage. Several references erroneously state that the P-63C also had a wingspan that was reduced by ten inches, but the official USAAF pilot's manuals, as well as

the erection and maintenance manual for each variant, all state that the span was 38' 4" for both versions. The large majority of P-63Cs were delivered to the Soviet Union, but 300 were provided to the Free French who used them for coastal patrols in Africa and Italy. Some French Kingcobras were still on hand for the fighting in Indochina in 1948.

The manned target version of the P-63C was the RP-63C-2-BE, and 200 were delivered to the USAAF. They were essentially the same as the previous RP-63As, except that they were powered by the P-63C's V-1710-117 engine. These aircraft also did not have the P-63C's usual ventral fin installed.

One P-63C was fitted with a second cockpit behind the engine, and it was redesignated the TP-63C. **(USAFM)**

DATA

Version	P-63C
Number Built	1,227
Armament	1 X 37-mm cannon, 4 x .50 caliber
Powerplant	Allison V-1710-117
Horsepower	1,355
Maximum Speed	410 mph at 25,000 feet
Rate of Climb	8.6 minutes to 25,000 feet
Ceiling	38,600 feet
Maximum Range	2,100 miles
Combat Range	320 miles
Wingspan	38 feet, 4 inches
Length	32 feet, 8 inches
Height	12 feet, 6.25 inches
Empty Weight	6,800 pounds
Gross Weight	8,800 pounds
Maximum Take-off Weight	10,700 pounds
Maximum Internal Fuel	128 gallons
Maximum External Fuel	225 gallons

P-63C COCKPIT DETAILS

Details on the upper instrument panel and forward left side of the cockpit in a P-63A are indicated by numbered callouts in this photograph taken from the aircraft's technical manual. Keys for the callouts are provided below. *(USAFM)*

1. Cabin Door Opening Handle
2. Clear Vision Windshield Panel
3. Engine Control Quadrant
4. Fluorescent Light
5. Emergency Door Release Lever
6. Landing Gear Warning Horn
7. Cabin Windshield Defroster Heater Tube
8. Parking Brake Handle
9. Gun Sight Filament Switch
10. Control Stick
11. Gun Sight
12. Fluorescent Light

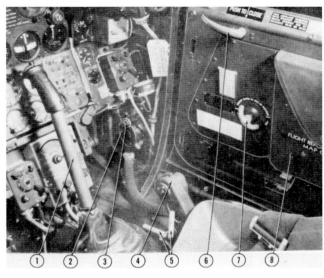

Features from the control column to the right side door are indicated here. The nomenclature of the items are listed in the keys below. *(USAFM)*

1. Control Stick
2. A-12 Oxygen Regulator
3. Oxygen Regulator Emergency Knob
4. Landing Gear Hand Crank
5. Wing Bombs Manual Release Handles
6. Cabin Door Opening Handle
7. Cabin Window Lowering Handle
8. Flight Report Holder and Map Case

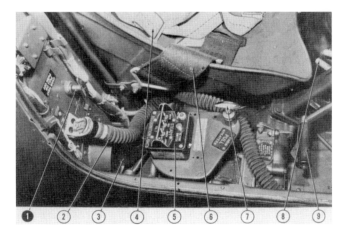

These details were located on or next to the right side of the seat. *(USAFM)*

1. Carburetor Heat Control (P-63-1-BE only)
2. Oxygen Mask Connector Tube
3. Cabin Heat Deflector Vanes
4. Pilot's Shoulder Harness
5. Recognition Lights Control Box
6. Pilot's Safety Belt
7. Cabin Heat Control Handle
8. Wing Bombs Manual Release Handles
9. Landing Gear Hand Crank

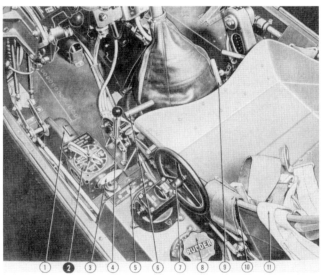

The items on the left side of the seat remained basically the same as those used on all versions of both the Airacobra and the Kingcobra. *(USAFM)*

1. Controls Lock
2. Fuel Selector Valve Control Handle
3. Defroster Control Handle
4. Center Panel Bomb Armed and Safe Lever
5. Aileron Trim Tab Control Switch
6. Center Panel Bomb Release Handle
7. Elevator Trim Tab Control
8. Rudder Trim Tab Control
9. Wing Bombs Manual Release Handles
10. Pilot's Safety Belt
11. Pilot's Shoulder Harness

Above and right: Two hundred P-63C-1-BEs were modified to be used as manned target aircraft, and they were redesignated RP-63C-2-BEs. They were similar to the previous RP-63As illustrated on page 60. Remaining RP-63Cs were redesignated QF-63C-2-BEs in 1948. **(Both USAFM)**

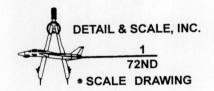

DETAIL & SCALE, INC.

1

72ND

● SCALE DRAWING

P-63C 1/72nd SCALE DRAWING

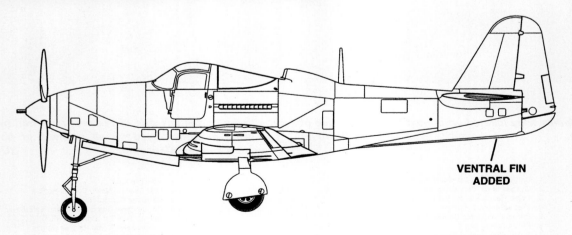

VENTRAL FIN
ADDED

DETAIL & SCALE, 1/72nd SCALE, COPYRIGHT © DRAWING BY LLOYD S. JONES

P-63E & P-63F

Thirteen P-63Es were completed as P-63E-1-BEs before the remaining 2,930 aircraft in the order, designated P-63E-5-BEs, were canceled. The P-63E-1s were powered by the V-1710-109 engine, and they had a different wing design than the one used on the P-63A or P-63C. This new wing design was also used on the sole P-63D. *(USAFM)*

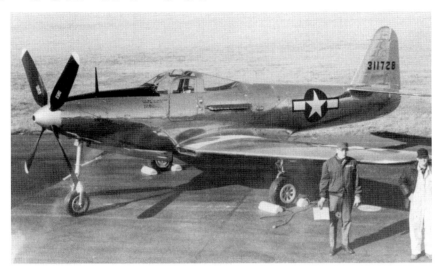

Only two P-63Fs were built. They were essentially the same as the P-63C, except that they had a taller vertical tail and rudder, and they were powered by a V-1710-135 engine. This is the first of the two P-63Fs, and the other was assigned the serial number 43-11720. *(USAFM)*

P-63F 1/72nd SCALE DRAWING

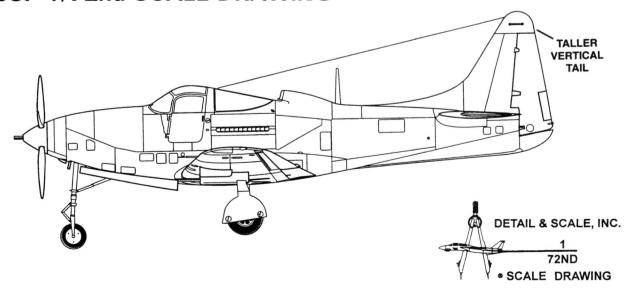

TALLER VERTICAL TAIL

DETAIL & SCALE, INC.

1
72ND
SCALE DRAWING

DETAIL & SCALE, 1/72nd SCALE, COPYRIGHT © DRAWING BY LLOYD S. JONES

RP-63G

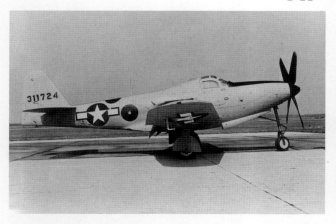

Above left and right: The final manned target version of the Kingcobra was the RP-63G, and thirty-two were built. They were similar to the RP-63C, but they were powered by the V-1710-135 engine which produced 1,425 horsepower. Lights, which flashed when the plane was hit with the frangible bullets, were installed on the fuselage and surrounded with large painted black discs.

(Both, USAFM)

Left: RP-63G, 45-57300, was fitted with an experimental V tail. Although it was quite successful, this tail was not used on any other Kingcobra.

(USAFM)

RP-63G 1/72nd SCALE DRAWING

DETAIL & SCALE, INC.

$\frac{1}{72ND}$

® SCALE DRAWING

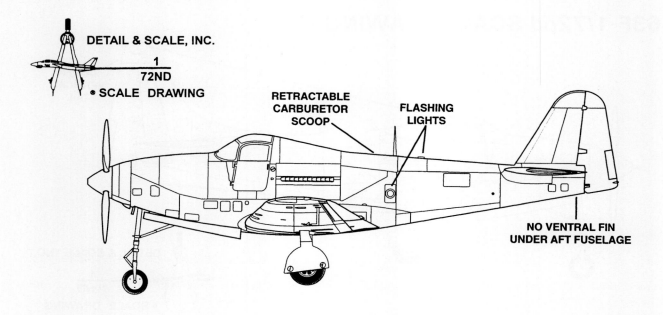

RETRACTABLE CARBURETOR SCOOP

FLASHING LIGHTS

NO VENTRAL FIN UNDER AFT FUSELAGE

DETAIL & SCALE, 1/72nd SCALE, COPYRIGHT © DRAWING BY LLOYD S. JONES

P-63 KINGCOBRA DETAILS
LANDING GEAR DETAILS

The nose gear used on the Kingcobra was similar to the one used on the Airacobra, but there were some minor detail differences. Most noticeable was that the oleo link was on front of the strut rather than on the back.

Like the Airacobra's nose gear, there was a small door mounted on front of the strut at the top. Two longer doors on the sides of the well covered the rest of the gear when it was retracted.

An interior view of the forward end of the nose gear well shows the contrast between the Bell green color on the strut and the Chromate Yellow Primer inside the well itself and on the inside surfaces of the doors. Also note the hinges that attached the doors to the well.

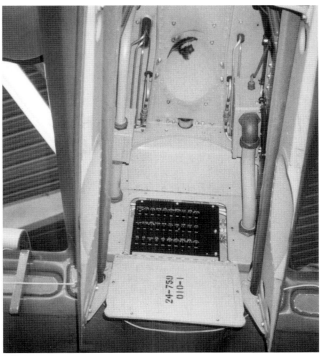

A black circuit breaker panel was located at the aft end of the nose gear well. As found on the Airacobra, the Kingcobra's nose gear well had a small depression at the aft end to provide ample clearance for the retracted tire. The aft hinges for the two side doors are also visible.

Above left: A front view of the left main landing gear shows the alignment of the strut and two gear doors.

Above right: Additional details of the left main gear are revealed in a view from the outside. Note the two small vents on the lower door as well as the hole that provides access to the axle bolt.

Below left: The strut was painted with the Bell green color, while the wheel was silver on both sides. The interior of the gear well and the inside surface of both doors was Chromate Yellow Primer.

Below right. A view looking inboard and up into the left gear well reveals that the Kingcobra did not have inner main gear doors like those used on the Airacobra.

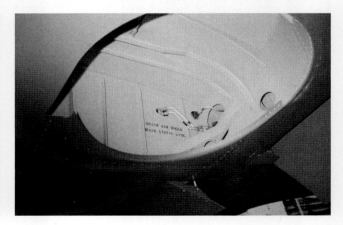

Above left: A close-up of the right main landing gear shows how the two doors overlapped to allow for the expansion and contraction of the gear strut.

Above right: Details on the inside of the right gear include the oleo link and the hydraulic brake line that ran down from the inside of the wing to the fitting on the wheel. Note the bend and slack in the line that allowed for the expansion of the gear.

Below left: The interior of the right main gear well is shown here. Again, note the lack of an inner gear door.

Below right: A look at outer part of the right gear well shows how the strut was attached inside the wing. The hydraulic line for the brake can be seen inside the well.

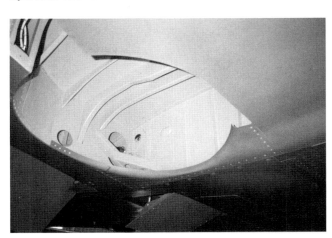

FUSELAGE DETAILS

Many Kingcobras, especially those delivered to the Soviet Union, had a connector on the tube that covered the cannon barrel. This connector served as a receptacle for a large crank on an auxiliary starter mounted on a truck. This auxiliary means of starting was especially helpful in extremely cold conditions.

Another view provides a different look at the receptacle for the starter. The notches were designed in such a way that they allowed the starter truck to easily disengage once the engine was turning the propeller. Details of the spinner are also shown in this photograph and the one to the left.

This stenciling and logo for the Aeroproducts Aeroprop was found on each blade of the propeller. The stenciling included the serial number of the blade, its name and nomenclature, and its low and high angles.

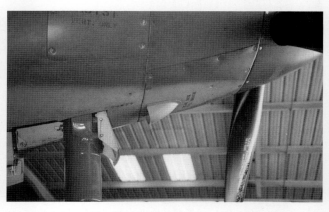

A small fairing covered the vent for the oil drain associated with the oil tank and system for the gear box that was located at the forward end of the nose section. Also note the small front gear door from this side angle.

As on the Airacobra, the Kingcobra had a chute on each side that retained spent shells from the .50-caliber machine guns. A door was located low on each side of the nose, and the spent shells could be emptied through it. These doors were larger than the comparable ones found on the P-39.

Details of the Kingcobra's cabin enclosure were very similar to those on the Airacobra. Stenciling on the door and the side of the fuselage is to official specifications. The Ethylene Glycol coolant was added through a filler on the fuselage side. It can be seen just aft of the door handle in this photograph.

The forward end of the radio antenna wire attached to a point on top of the rollover structure.

The carburetor air intake had a rectangular cross section instead of the oval design used on the Airacobra.

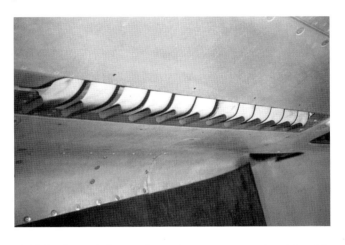

A high view of the twelve exhaust ports on the right side shows their flattened design.

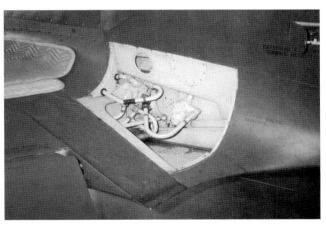

A cover could be removed from the aft end of the left wing root to provide access to these plumbing lines.

The receptacle for external electrical power was located on the left side of the fuselage at a point even with the trailing edge of the wing. The Kingcobra used a 24-volt electrical system.

Part of the gun sight alignment equipment and the overflow drain for the engine oil tank were under the aft fuselage. The drain cock for the oil return line is located to the right side of the aircraft near the wing filet.

WING DETAILS

The inlets that provided cooling air to the oil coolers and engine coolant radiator were buried in the wing roots. Note the smaller triangular shaped inlet inboard of the longer main inlet.

A divider inside each air inlet channeled air back to the engine coolant radiator inn the center of the aircraft and the two oil coolers, one of which was located on each side of the radiator for the engine coolant.

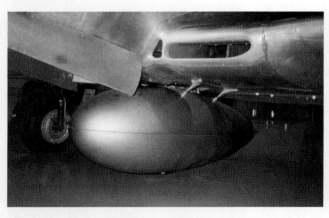

The external fuel tank was mounted almost flush with the underside of the aircraft. Two anti-sway braces held the tank steady in the airstream. Tanks of 64-gallon and 75-gallon capacities could be carried on this station.

A rear view reveals additional details of the external fuel tank as well as the vents for the three radiators. Airflow passing through the radiators was controlled by the three moveable flaps.

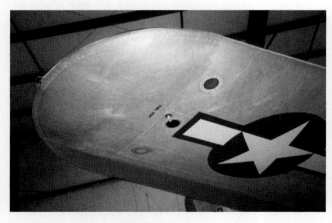

A single navigation light was mounted directly on the edge of each wing tip on the Kingcobra. This arrangement differed from the one used on the Airacobra, where there was one light on the top and one light on the bottom of each wing tip panel. The usual three identification lights remained under the right wing tip, and they are also visible in this photograph.

The pitot probe on the P-63 was located under the left wing, and it was this L-shaped design, rather than the long boom on the leading edge of the wing as used on the P-39. In some cases, the pitot probe was like the one shown here, with the vertical part being perpendicular to the wing. On many aircraft, the vertical part of the probe was angled back slightly from the wing.

The retractable landing/taxi light under the left wing of the P-39 was replaced by a much larger fixed unit in the leading edge of the wing on the P-63. It was almost directly in front of the left landing gear.

The ailerons were covered with metal instead of fabric as used on the Airacobra. Only the P-63C-1-BE and P-63C-5-BE had an adjustable trim tab for the ailerons.

The gun camera was mounted inside the right wing, and a small circular hole for its lens was in the leading edge of the wing.

The split flaps of the Airacobra were replaced with full flaps on the Kingcobra, but they were still operated by an electric motor. This is the right flap in the lowered position, and the maximum deflection was forty-five degrees.

On the Kingcobra, the fillers for the fuel tanks were further out on the wings than they were on the Airacobra. On this aircraft, the painted filler cap almost appears to be a red disc at the center of the national insignia.

An underside view provides a good look at additional details of the right flap in the lowered position. Note the lightening holes in the edge and the control arm at the center.

TAIL DETAILS

On P-63As, the rudder spanned the entire height of the vertical tail and fuselage.

When the fin was added under the tail of the P-63C, part of it extended under the rudder.

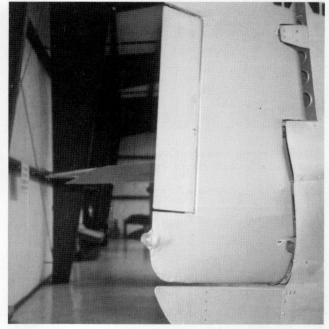

Left: The rudder was covered with fabric and the trim tab had an actuator on the left side.

Above: There was a white navigation light below the trim tab on the tailing edge of the rudder.

The antenna wire was attached to the leading edge of the vertical tail at a point just below the fin cap.

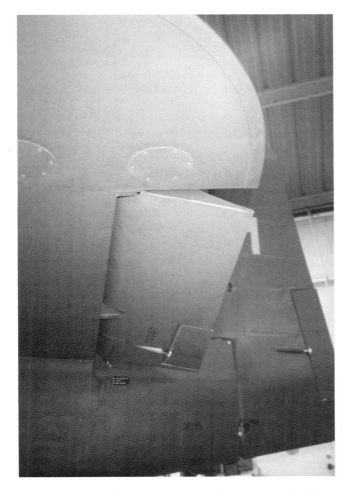

The elevators did not span the entire horizontal tail as they had on the P-39. The actuator for the trim tab on the left elevator was on the bottom surface.

P-39Cs had a long fin or strake added under the aft fuselage to increase longitudinal stability.

A moveable trim tab was on the left elevator only.

The right elevator had a fixed balance tab at its inboard end. The ailerons were metal covered, but the rudder and elevators were covered with fabric.

MODELERS SUMMARY

Note: Each volume in Detail & Scale's "In Detail" Series of publications has a Modelers Summary in the back of the book. The Modelers Summary will discuss the injection-molded plastic model kits of the aircraft covered by the book, and all common modeling scales from 1/144th through 1/32nd scale will be included. Highlights of the better kits in each scale will be discussed, and recommendations will be made with respect to which kit or kits in each scale are the best for the serious scale modeler to use. Once a kit has been purchased, the modeler should compare the various features of the kit to the drawings and photographs in the book to determine how accurately and extensively they are represented. He can then decide what, if any, correcting or detailing work he wants to do to enhance the appearance of the model.

GENERAL COMMENTS

Although there are several kits of the Airacobra and the Kingcobra in 1/72nd scale, none are better than average. Even the new P-39 from Academy has a number of significant inaccuracies. Although it is over twenty-five years old, the best model of the Airacobra remains the old Monogram 1/48th scale kit, now available from Revell-Monogram. All of the injection-molded 1/72nd scale and 1/48th scale models of the Kingcobra are limited run kits from foreign countries that fall far short of today's standards. There are no injection-molded plastic kits of the Airacobra or the Kingcobra in 1/32nd scale.

1/144th SCALE

The only 1/144th scale plastic model kit of the Airacobra that has been released is a P-39Q from Revell. It is generally accurate in shape and outline, but it lacks detail. Fortunately, the missing details are easily added from scrap plastic. The cockpit is simply an open hole in the fuselage, and with the Airacobra's large canopy, the addition of a floor, seat, instrument panel, and control column made from plastic card and stretched sprue will

The only plastic model kit of the Airacobra that has been released in 1/144th scale is this P-39Q from Revell. The author built this one to represent an aircraft from the 362nd Fighter Squadron of the 357th Fighter Group at Hayward Field, California.

add a lot to the appearance of the finished model. The inner main gear doors are also missing from the kit, and these can be made from thin plastic card. Finally, the pitot probe needs to be added from a very fine piece of stretched sprue. If these details are added, this kit can be completed as a nice little model of the P-39Q. If the gun pods are deleted, and stretched sprue or fine wire is used to add the .30-caliber wing guns, other variants of the Airacobra can be built.

Only one 1/144th scale plastic kit of the Kingcobra has been released, but it has been issued under both the Arii and Crown labels. Again, the basic shape of the model is generally accurate, but there are a few problems. The nose gear strut mounts into a hole that is slightly offset to the right, and there is no nose gear well. The nose gear strut has only a half fork on one side of the wheel rather than being the correct full fork design. The hole for the cockpit is tapered and the windscreen is rounded in front rather than being flat. The carburetor air intake is rounded on top, but it should be flat with a rectangular opening. Other problems include exhausts that are just a raised line on each side of the fuselage, and there are landing/taxi lights on both wings rather than just on the left. Two external fuel tanks are provided to go under the wings, but there are no pylons for them. The instructions show them being glued to the gun pods, but this is incorrect. The gun pods are also inaccurate, because the barrels are on the leading edge of the wings rather than being on the pods as they should be.

The wing to fuselage fit is very poor, and it will take a lot of filling and sanding to get it right. Care must also be taken when gluing the elevators to the horizontal stabilizers.

If the inaccuracies are corrected and some basic details are added in the open cockpit hole, a decent 1/144th scale model of the P-63A can be completed. It would also be relatively simple to add the fin under the tail to convert the model to a P-63C.

1/72nd SCALE

Early 1/72nd scale kits of the P-39 include releases from Revell, Airfix/MPC, and Heller. Neither the Revell nor Airfix/MPC kits can be considered by serious modelers because of their inaccuracies and lack of detailing. The Heller kit is a little better, and it was also issued by Testors. In either case, it still leaves much to be desired.

The best choice is the relatively new Academy kit which can be used to build any Airacobra variant from the P-39D through the P-39Q. However, it also has some significant problems. Academy did a poor job researching the P-39, and this resulted in some noticeable inaccuracies. The forward nose gear door is too large, and the nose gear strut is located too far aft in the well. It should be at the very front of the well. Both types of exhausts are included, but the ones with only six stubs are flat rather than having the correct circular cross section at the openings. The left cockpit door can be displayed in the open position, but it was the right side door usually used by pilots. The throttle is molded on the door, rather than being on the door jam where it should be. To make matters worse, there is a throttle on both doors. Noticeable

The best 1/72nd scale Airacobra is the Academy model, but it still has quite a few inaccuracies that need to be corrected. The author used kit decals on this model to build Lt. Col. Willam Shomo's well known "Snooks 2ⁿᵈ."

features missing from the cockpit include the trim knobs, wheel, and box on the left side of the seat and the handles on the right side.

The taper of the wing tips is not quite correct, and the two .30-caliber wing guns are even rather than being offset as they should be. The outer gun on each wing should be lower than the inboard gun.

To help correct and improve this kit, Verlinden Productions has released a detailing set. Although the box says it is for a Minicraft kit, Minicraft does not have a P-39 model. Evidently, Verlinden mistakenly thought that Academy and Minicraft were still working together, but the two companies ended their association some time ago. We highly recommend Verlinden's kit to correct inaccuracies and to significantly enhance the detailing of the Academy kit.

For the Kingcobra, there are three injection-molded 1/72nd scale kits, but the one by Aoshima is very crude and cannot be considered. Toko's kits of the P-63A and P-63C are molded in shiny gray plastic, and the clear parts look like they have been coated with wax. Surface detailing is an odd mix of engraved and raised lines as well as raised rivet detail. The doors are molded in clear plastic with some details represented on the inside surfaces. Detailing is reasonable in the cockpit and for the landing gear. Jim Roeder, who advises Detail & Scale on many kits, picks these Toko models as the best injection-molded Kingcobras in 1/72nd scale.

MPM has also released short run 1/72nd scale kits of the P-63A, P-63C, and RP-63. They are relatively basic kits with little detailing, and the fit is poor. The gear wells are open, and the cockpit only has a floor, seat, instrument panel, rollover structure, and the rear deck with a radio. The canopy is a vacuformed piece that has a very poor fit to the fuselage. Molding is not crisp, and most parts have some flash that will need to be removed.

We do not usually cover vacuformed kits in our Modelers Summary, but we suggest that modelers may want to consider the Wings vacuformed 1/72nd scale kits of the Kingcobra. They are well done and are really the best kits of the P-63 in any scale.

1/48th SCALE

In the 1950s, Revell issued a kit of the Airacobra in 1/45th scale that went on one of their well known "Revelling" stands that were popular during the early days of plastic modeling. Today, it is a collector's item. The only true 1/48th scale Airacobra that has ever been issued is the Monogram kit which has been released several times to represent different versions of the P-39 and the P-400. The most recent issue was from Revell-Monogram as a P-39Q in their ProModeler line of kits.

Although it is over twenty-five years old, this kit is excellent. It is quite accurate, and it has above average detailing. The right side cockpit door can be displayed in the open position, and there are also panels for the nose compartment and engine bay that can be displayed open to show detailing. Some small details are missing in the cockpit in most issues, but these were added with etched metal parts in the ProModeler release. The arms in the main gear wells that close the inner doors are also missing from the earlier releases, but they are included in the ProModeler issue as etched metal parts. When they are not included, it would be easy to make them from plastic rod and scrap plastic.

Although the surface detailing is raised, it is very fine, complete, and accurate. Even the control surfaces have a nicely represented fabric texture. In spite of its age, this is an excellent kit, and we strongly recommend it.

MPM has released short run kits of the Kingcobra in 1/48th scale that closely parallel their 1/72nd scale models. Through the use of resin parts, detailing is a little better, especially in the cockpit, but the gear wells remain open. Canopies are vacuformed, and one issue has the bubble canopy used on the P-63D and a single British Kingcobra as an option.

As on most limited run kits, the molding is not crisp, and the edges of all parts need cleaning up. Fit leaves a lot to be desired, so a lot of filling and sanding is required.

Wings has excellent vacuformed P-63s in 1/48th scale, and considering the lack of quality in the MPM injection-molded kits, modelers who are willing to work with vacuformed kits may want to use the Wings models instead.

Although it is over twenty-five years old, the Monogram 1/48th scale kit of the Airacobra is quite good. Stan Parker used an early issue to build this model of "HAWK EYE," a P-400 from the 41ˢᵗ Fighter Squadron of the 35ᵗʰ Fighter Group. **(Parker)**

More In Detail Titles from squadron/signal publications....

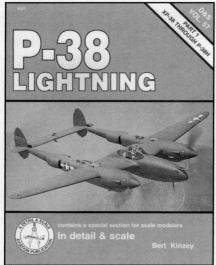

8257 P-38 Lightning Part 1

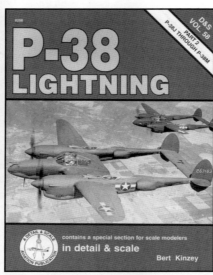

8258 P-38 Lightning Part 2

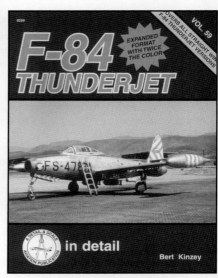

8259 F-84 Thunderjet

8260 B-25 Mitchell

8261 P-40 Warhawk Part 1

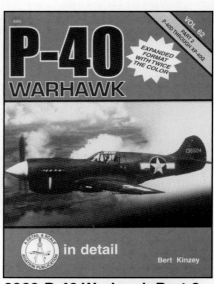

8262 P-40 Warhawk Part 2

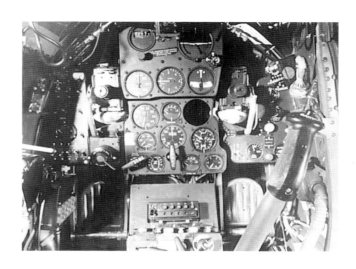

The engine gage unit has been removed from the instrument panel in this P-39Q, but otherwise all of the features are illustrated. The aft ends of the two .50-caliber machine guns are clearly visible as well. *(USAFM)*

Errata,
Unfortunately the photo on page 28 and the drawings on page 30 and 31 were printed in error. Please accept our apology.

Squadron Signal Publications

P-39Q, 1/72nd SCALE, FIVE-VIEW DRAWINGS

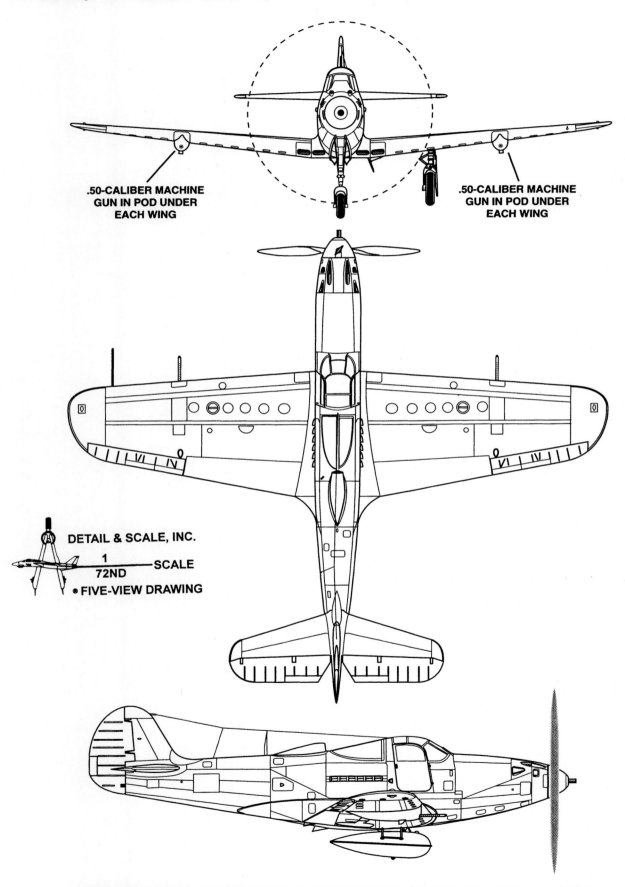

.50-CALIBER MACHINE GUN IN POD UNDER EACH WING

.50-CALIBER MACHINE GUN IN POD UNDER EACH WING

DETAIL & SCALE, INC.

1
——— SCALE
72ND

● FIVE-VIEW DRAWING

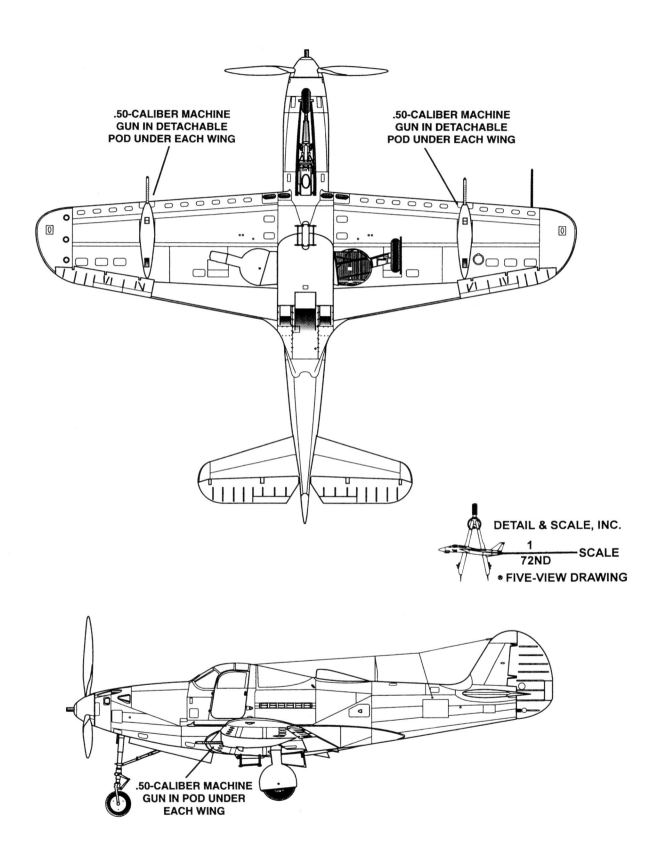

.50-CALIBER MACHINE
GUN IN DETACHABLE
POD UNDER EACH WING

.50-CALIBER MACHINE
GUN IN DETACHABLE
POD UNDER EACH WING

DETAIL & SCALE, INC.

$$\frac{1}{72ND}$$ SCALE

● FIVE-VIEW DRAWING

.50-CALIBER MACHINE
GUN IN POD UNDER
EACH WING